MicroExploring the SuperSanctuary

The peace and joy
of nature await you!

Ignacio

Spoonwood Pond and the surrounding landscape of the SuperSanctuary in its fall finest.

Photo by Eric Aldrich

MicroExploring the SuperSanctuary

15 Mindful Meanders

in New Hampshire's Monadnock Region

PHIL BROWN & IGNACIO OREAMUNO

THE DREAMCATCHERS

Cover and back cover design and photography by Phil Brown and Ignacio Oreamuno
except back cover group photo by Ben Conant and loon photo by Brian Reilly;
cover model: Olivia Turcotte

Published by The Dreamcatchers

The Dreamcatchers is an experiential nature-based company that creates immersive journeys built around personal growth, conservation, and the art of letting go. Our custom experiences invite travelers to release control and step into wonder, allowing the natural world, flow, and the present moment to guide the experience.

www.thedreamcatchers.co

ISBN: 979-8-218-90926-0
Printed in the United States by Gasch Printing

First Edition
10 9 8 7 6 5 4 3 2 1

Book Team
Project manager: Tim Ditlow
Editor: John Knight / Copy editor: Hannah Mahoney
Proofreader: Henry Walters / Indexer: Joe Bills
Design: Gwarlingo Studio (Corwin Levi & Michelle Aldredge)

Fonts include Drummond Variable, Futura PT, Minion Pro, and Roboto

To my family:

Dad, my top advisor, an encouraging voice, thoughtful critic, and guiding inspiration through all my endeavors; Mom, my biggest fan; and Chris, the trailblazer for my own journeys.

Laurel and Alden, for helping me see the world in a new light.

And Julie, my original companion on these journeys.

PB

To my daughter, Amalia, who grew up wandering with me through these beautiful and magical forests. The memories we made here are the best part of my life! ♥ Amo

IO

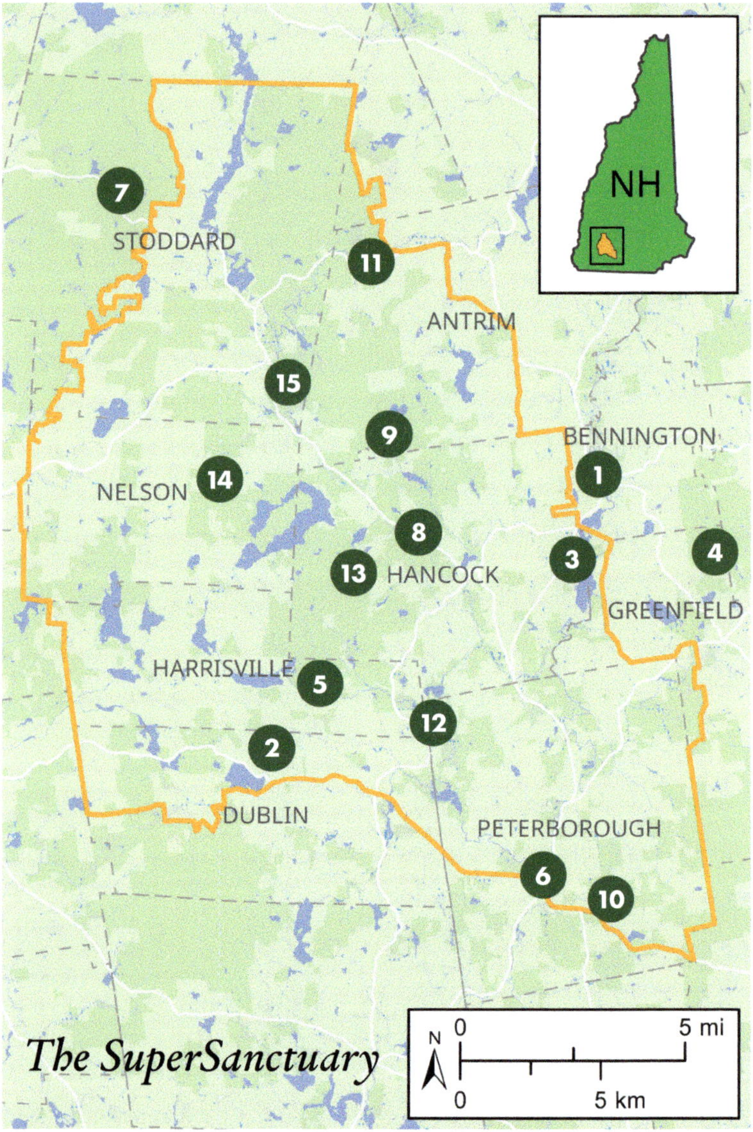
NH
STODDARD
ANTRIM
BENNINGTON
NELSON
HANCOCK
GREENFIELD
HARRISVILLE
DUBLIN
PETERBOROUGH
1
2
3
4
5
6
7
8
9
10
11
12
13
14
15
N
0
5 mi
0
5 km
The SuperSanctuary

CONTENTS

FOREWORD

It is not surprising that Phil Brown and Ignacio Oreamuno have created a guide to the remarkable landscape of the southwestern highlands of New Hampshire. Since the early 2020s, they have been leading programs they call "Mindful Meanderings through MicroExploring" for the Harris Center for Conservation Education, the home base of the SuperSanctuary. With a devoted following, these two guides have been crafting multisensory experiences in nature that always leave people hungry for more. Now, with *MicroExploring the SuperSanctuary*, Phil and Ignacio are giving each of us the tools to become our own guides and explore our natural world not only with our feet, but with our hearts fully engaged and senses newly heightened.

From high mountaintops and granite ledges to winding rivers and hidden bogs, there are discoveries to be made at every turn in the SuperSanctuary. With almost forty-four thousand acres of protected land touching nine towns, the SuperSanctuary is just what Meade Cadot had hoped to create when he was the Harris Center's director, from 1975 to 2009. He saw firsthand how quickly wild landscapes could vanish at the hands of large-scale development. During the development boom of the early 1980s, he witnessed family farms and forests disappear in Nashua, New Hampshire, just thirty-five miles from the Harris Center, while box stores and shopping malls grew in their place. It was a vivid reminder of what had happened to his childhood woods and wetlands. Meade grew up wandering along the lush estuaries, rivers, and woodlands of northern Delaware in the

1950s and '60s. He'd watched as almost all of it disappeared, paved over to make way for shops and industry. His favorite places to watch birds were gone, and so were the birds. This childhood loss set his course, motivating him to pursue a career in natural sciences. He has dedicated his life to fighting for land protection and working to prevent the devastating impact of habitat fragmentation and loss. As the director of the Harris Center for almost forty years, Meade was a sentinel, standing strong and always working to make sure the Monadnock region didn't trade its wild lands for profit but rather invested in nature for the future of all who would come after him.

Slowly and steadily, the Harris Center has worked alongside other conservation partners, including land trusts, nongovernmental organizations, and local, state, and federal partners, stitching together a quilt of contiguous protected lands, creating a habitat where animals like bobcats, moose, fishers, and bears have room to roam, a place where the songs of insects and birds mark out the morning, and the scent of spring wildflowers sweetens the air.

And none of this remarkable story of land protection could have happened if it hadn't been for the philanthropic power and vision of the Harris Center's founder, Eleanor Briggs. As a young girl, Eleanor would often visit and stay at her grandparents' estate in Hancock. Coming from Long Island, she always looked forward to resting her head on the soft moss in the quiet woods around her family home. She found it peaceful, and as she grew, she sought solace and found company in the solitude of the woods. She, like Meade, was witnessing the changing landscape of her Long Island home during the 1960s. The wild places that she loved to explore were being bulldozed to make room for homes, stores, and businesses.

In 1966, when Eleanor was twenty-nine, her father sold the Hancock estate, which spanned three thousand acres, to a developer. As Eleanor recalls, "Remembering what happened to my childhood home on Long Island . . . I began to visualize skyscrapers around Norway Pond. One morning, I woke up with a jolt of anxiety and decided the only way to calm down was to do something about my fears." By 1970, Eleanor had bought back all the land that had belonged to her grandparents, and she didn't stop there.

Ahead of her time, Eleanor recognized that people need ample time and personal experiences in nature to be motivated to protect and care for the natural world. She wanted everyone to have the opportunity to find the peace and power she experienced in the mossy woods. In 1970, Eleanor helped found the Harris Center, a place that would come to protect so many acres for wildlife and people. For over fifty years, the Harris Center hasn't only been protecting land. It has also been helping to build deep and lasting relationships between people and communities with the natural world out their back door and in their towns. At the core of the Harris Center and its SuperSanctuary lies the belief that we all can fall in love with this wild world.

MicroExploring the SuperSanctuary shares the same hope. With detailed walk descriptions, sensory prompts, and personal reflections, this book is both a trail guide and a mindfulness companion. It's about how to slow down your hike, open your senses, and discover what makes a place special. Although it highlights the SuperSanctuary in New Hampshire's Monadnock region, it is a blueprint for how to explore and fall in love with any place in our world. Put what you learn from this book into your own heart and soul and bring it with you wherever you go.

Susie Spikol
Writer and naturalist

Eleanor Briggs with Susie Spikol at the Harris Center.

MicroExploring
the SuperSanctuary

INTRODUCTION

Let's be honest—most guidebooks miss the mark. They're clinical, impersonal, obsessed with the highest peaks, most popular hikes, and postcard views; they often demand long drives, full packs, and endless stamina, only to deliver a crowded summit. They teach the route, not the reverence.

MicroExploring is not just about *where* to walk, but also *how* to walk.

This one is different. It's not just about *where* to walk, but also *how* to walk. It's not about conquering peaks; it's about noticing what's underfoot, overhead, and all around us. It's about restoring something most of us have lost: a deep, sensory connection to the natural world. It's about discovering trails and small patches of woods, brooks, wetlands, and fields right where we are. It's about moving slowly, paying attention, engaging all the senses, and allowing ourselves to feel joy, curiosity, and awe. It's about finding meaning not in faraway wilderness but in the everyday wild. We call it MicroExploring, and we think of it as the practice of embracing the overlooked.

Adopt the pace of nature to discover its many hidden treasures.

MicroExploring is the intentional, ongoing exploration of the nature and geography within a short radius of our homes—often no more than a ten- or fifteen-minute walk, bike, or drive away. It's guided by wonder, not agenda. It's the art of noticing what's right in front of us: trails, rivers, hidden views, quiet town corners. It's about keeping an appointment with the season, taking the same walk twice, and discovering novelty just beyond our doorsteps. The best part is that MicroExploring is for everyone and can be practiced anywhere. Regardless of your experience level—whether you're a seasoned hiker or a curious beginner—MicroExploring offers you a doorway. Not just to the outdoors but also to a kind of aliveness. A way to inhabit the world—not as a tourist but as a participant with fresh eyes.

This book outlines a series of hikes and practices rooted in the almost forty-four thousand acres of conserved landscape of southwestern New Hampshire known as the SuperSanctuary. Whether you call this region home or are a visitor, this book will help you learn, celebrate, and connect more deeply with this spectacular corner of the Granite State.

MicroExploring is not about chasing peaks; it is about embracing a childlike wonderment to connect with what is right in front of us.

How MicroExploring Discovered Us

Place blindness is the tendency to overlook what's always around us. When a place becomes too familiar, we stop seeing it. Its beauty fades into the background, and our curiosity dries up. We soon start chasing novelty, thinking the extraordinary lies elsewhere. When you're not chasing epic views or top-ten lists, almost anything becomes worth discovering: a brook you didn't know existed; a view of your town from a rock outcrop you've never stood on; a forgotten trail that ends at a beaver dam; the texture of a rock wall hidden in the woods; the song of a bird you've never heard before; an old cellar hole. It's like being a kid again, limited only by how far your bike can take you.

As fathers living in this region, both of us have been exploring the SuperSanctuary alone, together, and with our kids for years. Our friendship grew from experiences walking its trails, paddling its waters, and biking its back roads and rail trails. Embracing nature became our way of balancing life, destressing, and connecting with a healthy natural environment around us. When the pandemic hit, we began homeschooling our young kids. Each Monday, we got our families together for little adventures in our own backyards and beyond—observing birds and tracking mammals, paddling rivers and lakes by canoe, swimming in brooks and ponds, creating art and music in nature—all while supporting a safe and fun space for us all.

As we kept exploring, we discovered more secrets. It was as if the land started revealing itself to us. Abandoned farms rich with stories and forgotten woods roads. Massive glacial boulders and ancient trees tucked deep in forests. Seldom-seen wildlife, bountiful blooms, and spectacular summits. We became more grounded, building a mental map of the land around us and amassing a deeper knowledge of its landscapes. Our small town began to feel boundless.

The more we wandered close to home, the more we felt it: this was a new kind of exploration. Closer. Slower. Quieter. It didn't have a name. So we gave it one: MicroExploring. At some point, we realized we were living inside an idea that had the power to do real good beyond our own families. In 2022, we began leading our first MicroExploring walks—guiding people through overlooked trails and hidden gems all over the SuperSanctuary. The response was powerful. These walks weren't just pleasant diversions; they were helping people feel better—mentally, physically, and emotionally.

The SuperSanctuary

Most visitors to the region hike the popular trails or climb Mount Monadnock, its most notable feature, but there's so much more. The SuperSanctuary is bounded largely by Routes 9, 202, and 101, and you can drive its perimeter in just a couple of hours. But it'll take you years to fully explore all its trails, natural areas, and conserved landscapes.

The term SuperSanctuary was coined by Meade Cadot of the Harris Center for Conservation Education in the 1980s; it essentially describes clustered undeveloped landscapes. Its guiding conservation principle is based on the premise that a cluster of

The Harris Center in Hancock, heart and home to many of our favorite trails and conserved lands.

protected parcels has greater conservation value than an equal number of parcels randomly distributed across the landscape.

The SuperSanctuary, which extends over nine towns in southwestern New Hampshire, contains some of the most breathtaking conserved lands in New England. It is home to abundant wildlife and plant communities, and threaded throughout are stories about place and connection to the land. Its protected mosaic of forests, fields, wetlands, and waterways exists thanks to the dedication and long-standing efforts of many individuals and organizations that have worked tirelessly to conserve beloved natural areas, one property at a time.

Indigenous Presence and Continuity

Throughout this book, we highlight traces of history visible in the landscape—old stone walls, cellar holes, and fields once cleared for sheep-raising. We also wish to recognize and celebrate the deep Indigenous presence on these lands and the enduring vitality of the Abenaki peoples of this region.

For countless generations, Abenaki communities have lived in close relationship with this landscape—fishing in its waters, hunting in its forests, gathering plants for food and medicine, cultivating crops, and embodying their culture through story, art, and tradition.

Today, Abenaki people of this region continue to revitalize language, cultural practices, and community life, much of which had been lost to the impacts of colonization by Europeans. We encourage readers to learn more by reading Robert G. Goodby's book listed in the Further Resources section and and by attending local powwows, lectures, and cultural events.

As we walk these trails and meander through the forests, fields, and rivers of the Monadnock region, may we carry an awareness of the Indigenous past, present, and future that continue to shape and sustain this remarkable landscape.

The forests hold the echoes of many stories lived by both humankind and nature across millennia.

How to Use This Book

This book is our way of welcoming you into some of our most intimate curated pathways within the SuperSanctuary. Each walk offers something: a lesson, a vision, or a moment of peace. Each chapter introduces a walk or paddle accompanied by maps, practices, and reflections to draw you deeper into the way of MicroExploring. Together, these elements are meant to help you discover a deeper understanding of wherever you wander—and an unbounded version of yourself.

Celebrate the ordinary. Make your own discoveries. Go to the pond less paddled, the trail less hiked. Take the same walk twice. Don't always assign a name to a bird or a place. Walk with a friend or go solo. Take a night walk whenever you can. Be joyful, curious, and playful. Celebrate the seasons. Seek out flowing water and let it do the talking. Follow tracks. Look closely and move with intention. Bring good snacks!

The book's fifteen hand-selected routes include rugged ridgeline hikes, accessible hilltop viewpoints, and shoreline nature walks. There are gentle wetland paddles, biking routes, and even an urban immersion. All these places encourage public access, and some offer universal-access trails. They are free of charge, intentionally stewarded, and have ample parking.

Most importantly, each exploration is truly spectacular and unique. Though many are seemingly ordinary places, each one holds extraordinary stories, history, viewpoints, and natural spectacles.

Paired with each hike are what we've titled "MicroExploring Practices"—our insights into various practical wellness aspects associated with each outing. The framework we share here is the result of years of immersion and observation, the foundations that make our own time in nature come alive. They're simple to implement, fun to learn, and rewarding to share. The practices woven into each chapter blend the practical with the spiritual, turning even ordinary outings into moments of personal discovery, growth, and renewal.

While this book is rooted in New Hampshire, the approach can be applied anywhere. Whether you live in a city, suburb, or deep in the woods, there are trails, alleys, hidden corners, and wild surprises to be found close to home. Carry this book with you and use it as you explore. Allow it to open doors—into landscapes near and far, with a fresh perspective.

MicroExploring with Kids

Kids are natural MicroExplorers. Unbounded by expectations and the allure of the distant, they often immerse themselves in whatever is right in front of them. We can all stand to learn from their approach and be a little more childlike in our search for joy, wonder, and appreciation. MicroExploring with children is also an investment in the next generation of well-informed, nature-literate people, and it is the best way to ensure they will learn to love and steward our land and resources. Many of the hikes featured in this book are compatible with a child's approach to exploration. Regardless of your age, it's best to start small with easy and moderate hikes and build up to something more ambitious, if you so wish.

The search for accessible, easy-to-reach nature adventures with our children planted the seed for our MicroExploring adventures.

Safety Considerations and Gear

Many of the outings featured are shorter, front-country locations, but others are fairly remote and rugged. In any outdoor situation, one must be prepared in the case of an emergency. Falls, exposure (hypothermia, heat exhaustion), biting insects, poison ivy, and weather are some of the hazards to be aware of. Adequate preparation and common sense will go a long way in protecting you and your MicroExploring companions. MicroExplore with others whenever possible, and always let someone know where you're going. Finally, always heed the guidelines of relevant land-holding agencies and organizations, as this ensures access for all of us.

MicroExploring is designed to be easy, enjoyable, and repeatable so you can quickly mobilize whenever your soul needs it—like an old-school firefighter sliding down the pole: minimal fuss, maximum speed. When your gear is always ready, it minimizes the mental friction of having to think about logistics and supplies. Assemble a personalized adventure deployment system near your door with all the essentials you want in your day pack. You're now ready to answer that spontaneous call to adventure. It will create a habit—and eventually, a way of life.

Gear List

- Small lightweight day pack
- First aid kit (bandages, antiseptic wipes, pain relievers, etc.)
- Headlamp or flashlight (even for daytime walks!)
- Water (always bring more than you think you'll need!)
- High-energy food
- Pocket knife or multi-tool
- Sunscreen and sunglasses
- Insect repellent or bug net
- Extra layers (a light rain jacket or fleece, etc.)
- Hat (for sun and warmth)—blaze orange recommended during hunting season
- Binoculars or camera
- Thermos with warm beverage
- Walking stick or trekking pole
- Map and compass/GPS
- Whistle
- Fully charged phone (and portable power bank)
- Small trash bag
- Hand sanitizer
- Small notebook and pen/pencil
- Identification and emergency contact information

OSPREY
ULTRALIGHT / WATERTIGHT
MEDICAL KIT .7
FIELD
NOTES

Why Are We Giving Away Our Secrets?

We wrote this book because we've lived it. We've walked these paths with our kids, our friends, and each other. We've returned to the same brooks and fields through seasons of joy, illness, uncertainty, and calm. We've led others on these paths and watched something awaken in them, too. The goal of this book is to inspire people to walk mindfully and invite them to deepen their understanding and appreciation of the land. To notice more. To feel something. And ultimately, to act—because love of place leads naturally to care for place. In the words of Baba Dioum, a Senegalese forestry engineer, "In the end we will conserve only what we love, we will love only what we understand, and we will understand only what we are taught."

Photo by Lucy Zukaitis

May this book be a welcome guide for you to connect with nature, others, and yourself. Welcome to *MicroExploring the SuperSanctuary*. Let's begin our journey.

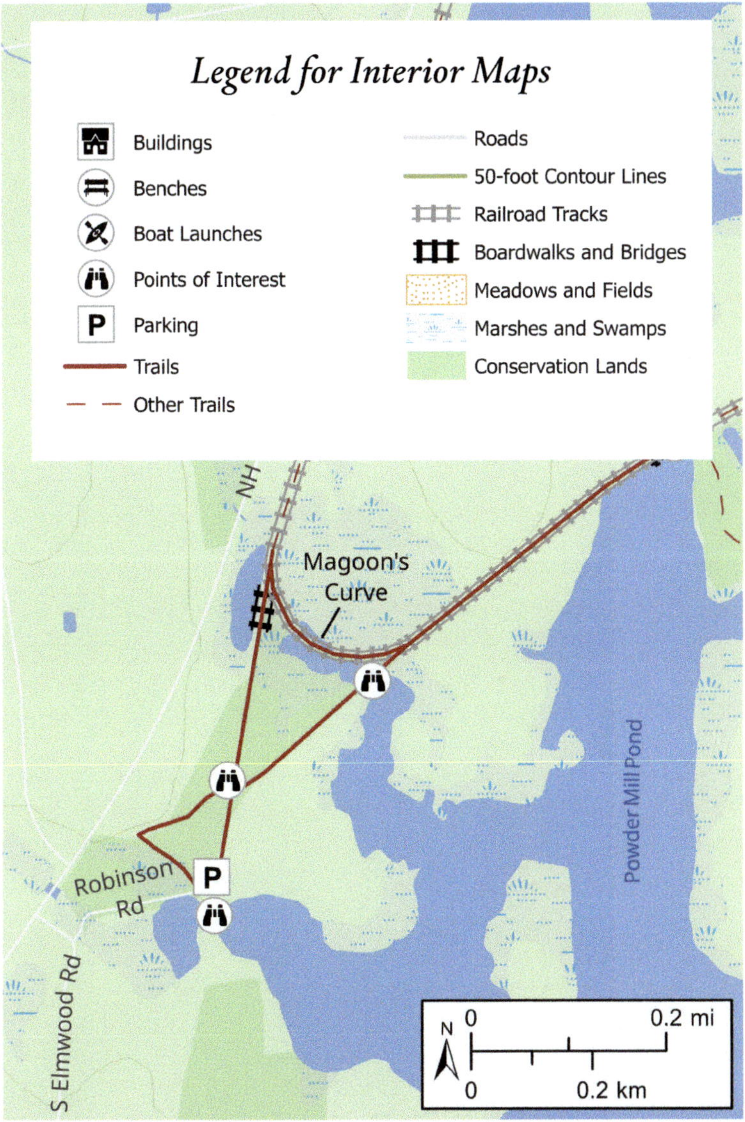

Legend for Interior Maps
Buildings
Benches
Boat Launches
Points of Interest
Parking
Trails
Other Trails
Roads
50-foot Contour Lines
Railroad Tracks
Boardwalks and Bridges
Meadows and Fields
Marshes and Swamps
Conservation Lands
NH
Magoon's Curve
P
Robinson Rd
S Elmwood Rd
Powder Mill Pond
N
0
0.2 mi
0
0.2 km

MicroExploring the SuperSanctuary

15 Mindful Meanders

in New Hampshire's Monadnock Region

PHIL BROWN & IGNACIO OREAMUNO

The rivers flow not past, but through us.

—John Muir

BRUCE EDES MEMORIAL FOREST 1
LEARNING TO OBSERVE

Riverside Wonders

Bennington

Walk Summary

A short walk from downtown Bennington, a historic and current mill town, is a small forest with big trees along the fast-flowing Contoocook River. A sizable trail network provides explorers with a variety of ways to experience railroad and mill history in a setting that nature now reclaims. The Bruce Edes Memorial Forest is a place to come when you want to walk, sit, and listen.

Highlights

- Feel the rush of water's power as you sit peacefully by the falls
- Wrap your arms around huge pines that somehow escaped the axe
- Decipher the history of a forest by reading clues from its trees and stone walls
- Admire hobblebush flowers and spring ephemerals along the river
- Listen to the roar of the natural falls just downstream from the paper mill they power

Hidden in plain sight near a rural town center is a tiny gem—a big forest that persists despite its proximity to roads, a railroad, several dams, and a paper mill. The forest's inviting trails meander along impressive natural and dammed waterfalls, weave through tall pine and hemlock forests, and offer a quick escape.

The Native American symbol of the four winds adorns trail markers along these paths. The circle represents the circle of life, and the four lines the cardinal directions.

A trailhead kiosk and picnic table make for a good meeting point; be sure to read the historical sign about the old mills. The sound of the river, especially after heavy rains or a spring melt, is immediate and relentless. It fills your ears, your chest; you can feel it shake the ground underfoot. The Contoocook River now powers the nearby paper mill. For thousands of years, it was the lifeline of the Pennacook people, a group within the Abenaki. It was a travel route, connecting villages and enabling trade. It also provided fish and other foodstuffs, and crops were cultivated along its shore.

Before setting out on the trail, walk out onto the bridge (via the sidewalk on the parking lot side) to view the river and two of the dams. Notice the high tree diversity right around the trailhead—paper and black birches, a Norway maple, a few elms, oaks, and a planted tupelo (black gum). Walk along the railroad tracks to access all the trails.

This forest is perfect for exploring and finding awe in the ordinary. Just down the trail from the kiosk, sit at the first of several well-placed Leopold benches. These small benches invite reflection and are based on an ingeniously simple design by Aldo Leopold, author and ecologist who is credited as the father of modern wildlife management. Here, an old American beech tree, its bark carved by teens from different generations, provides shade. Sit here to take in the morning sun and

If you have just five minutes for a Micro-Exploration, pause to take in the power of the falls.

admire the flow of pounding water. The sound drowns out the roar of trucks and the entire outside world, and perhaps that's the same relief people have sought here over the years.

From the bench, get your first glimpse of Crotched Mountain rising in the distance. Just across town, it's home to a rehabilitation center, ski slopes, fine hiking trails, and the site of the world's first commercial wind farm in 1980.

Continue along the tracks and look closely for small metal buttons hammered into the ties. The numbers indicate the year they were added, a type of graffiti of its time, one might think, but now a useful historical marker. Ponder what life was like in this bustling mill town during the years represented on the buttons: 1938, 1942 . . .

Let the River Guide You

Continuing on, you'll find a story trail that leads young readers through the woods. This feature rotates seasonally, thanks to the care of volunteers from the town library. Follow the trail marked by white circles, which hugs the river and stays in the morning sunlight—a feature you may find scarce later on. Across the river, a few houses peek through, but from late spring through early fall, leaves draw a curtain of green that provides solitude. Pass under a small power-line corridor, where oaks (and their abundance of caterpillar and insect dwellers) attract warblers in spring and fall. Lowbush blueberries grow along the path and ripen in July.

At the confluence of waters, a lush floodplain comes to life (Canada mayflower and wood anemone bloom abundantly in early May), and little footpaths kept fresh by anglers and beavers allow access to placid stretches of water. Here stands a lone spreading white pine, once the tallest in its clearing, now matched in height but not presence by younger red pines, their flaky reddish bark shining in sunlight. They were still healthy as of spring 2025, but a scale insect now threatens their survival due to a changing climate. In the woods nearby, research is being conducted by the local elementary school, with students focused on salamander habitat and mammal signs.

Bald eagles are a frequent sight along the river and in the tall pines.
Photo by Chuck Carlson

The main trail swings briefly away from the river and into a stretch where the road becomes audible again. But a narrow footpath leads right, hugging the water's edge and crossing a small wooden bridge over a wetland. You may have to duck beneath the fallen trunks of wind-thrown pines, reminders that nothing stands forever. At the trail's end, a wide concrete dam opens into the sun again. It's the last of the open light before the forest deepens once more. This is a good place to scan for ospreys and eagles—fish eaters that nest nearby. Back near the railroad tracks, you'll find two towering dead white pines, twins separated by the tracks, relics of history. Their blond inner wood shines in the sun.

There Are Many Paths

If you're short on time, return via the tracks, just a quarter mile. Otherwise, keep walking. The white-marked trail leads on, and soon you'll reach a junction: go left following the yellow circles for a faster loop, or onward following the white markers if you want more river. The yellow trail wanders through tall conifers. Many of the white pines show weevil damage, evidenced by the presence of multiple stems halfway up the trunk and a sign that they grew from former fields.

A series of stone walls in the forest's interior is somewhat baffling. The walls form a square and feature openings that are perfectly aligned with the directions of a compass. The area is mainly free from stones, indicating it likely had been cleared for cropland. But the square's origins and the reasons for its orientation aren't fully understood.

Find another bench here and observe a red pine stand—which takes the old field's place—likely planted by the Civilian Conservation Corps in the 1930s, when white pine was believed to be in decline. Today, this stand is thinning, and a new hardwood understory rises to take its place. Tune in to the song of summer birds here—the musical ringing of pine warblers; loud, clear whistles of chickadees and titmice; and the drumming of woodpeckers.

Though the forest is just thirty-four acres, the trail configurations feel endless. Spur trails branch out in many directions: the green trail leads right to the tracks, the orange goes left through hemlocks and boulder fields toward the white loop. The yellow trail climbs gently and is wide, inviting company. In the years to come, more light may reach this path as the older canopy opens. But across a stone wall, the forest shows signs of older age with widely spaced pines and a rocky, open understory. We call this type of older forest "creeper woods," referring to the tiny songbird that blends in with the trees' bark. In summer, black-throated green warblers sing from the canopy and ovenbirds belt out their songs from the understory.

Get tactile with ancient giants . . . they have many stories to share.

Near the height of land on the right stands a massive pine that forks like an oak. It's been here awhile, but how much longer it will hold up is anyone's guess. Red oaks here show coppiced trunks, indicating trees that grew back from cut stumps. We challenge you to find such recent logging evidence in this old forest. A red trail junction offers a choice: left back to the lot or right for one last view.

The Draw of the River

If time allows, take the white-marked trail left; it will bring you toward the river. Let its sound guide you. A bench facing the Monadnock Paper Mills soon appears. You can't see much, but you might hear the whistle that blows thrice daily—at seven a.m., noon, and five p.m.—an orienting feature for the several towns within earshot. Common mergansers and spotted sand-pipers, daredevils of the rushing river, forage at the edge of rapids. Ferns, hellebore, and other riparian (shoreline) plants emerge along the river's edge in early spring, and the brilliant white flowers of hobblebush shrubs appear in early May.

At a large glacial boulder, take the gold spur along the river a few hundred feet past ironwood trees (whose trunks and branches resemble bulging muscles) to a bench at the trail's terminus. Surrounded by a lovely stand of hobblebush, the bench faces the land that Bruce Edes cared for so meticulously as longtime property manager for the mill. He was a dedicated Bennington resident who worked to make a difference on many levels. The gold trail honors him. An institution and force for local good for over two hundred years, the paper mill donated much of the land to the town.

Back on the white trail, a stone wall leads to several behemoth white pines, some easily four feet in diameter and over 120 feet tall. Though not old growth, they give an impression of a forest left alone for a long time, and it is rare to see such large trees in the East.

The trail jogs left to the intersection with the red loop. Stay right at the boulder pile, which is fun for kids to explore. One final bench is perched atop the next rise. When the trees are leafless, you can sit here and enjoy the view of Crotched Mountain, the falls, and downtown Bennington. End as you began, with a seat and listening to the sound of yesterday and today.

Descend steeply on the white trail, careful not to slip on fallen oak leaves and acorns. The railroad tracks appear after a sign, and in moments, you're back at the lot.

Following the abandoned railroad tracks will bring you to a variety of optional paths full of possibilities. Look closely at the tracks to discover iron buttons stamped with numbers commemorating a succession of years, marking the passage of time in the railroad's history.

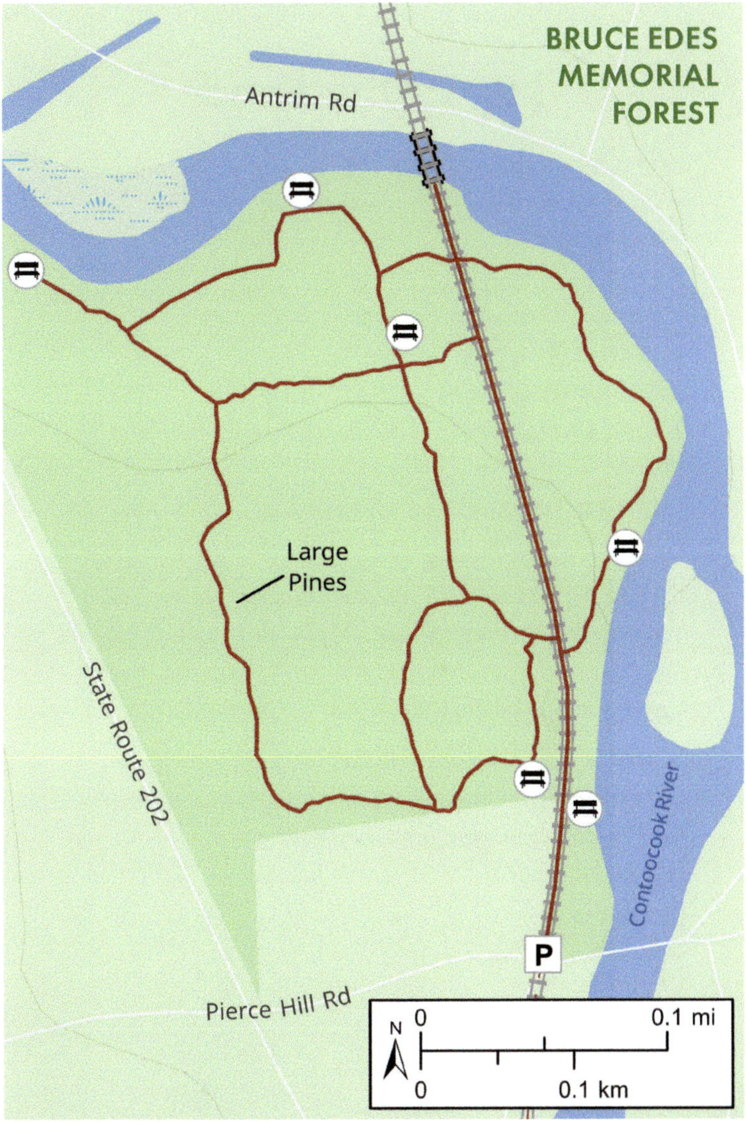
BRUCE EDES
MEMORIAL
FOREST
Antrim Rd
Large
Pines
State Route 202
Contoocook River
P
Pierce Hill Rd
N
0
0.1 mi
0
0.1 km

Lay of the Land

TRAILS: 2.1 miles of trails with several shorter loops; easy to moderate with some rocky sections and exposed roots

ACCESS: Parking area at the VFW building along Pierce Hill Road near downtown Bennington

PERMITTED USES: Foot traffic only; dogs OK on short leash at all times

A GREAT PLACE TO: Sit peacefully beside a raging river

INSIDER TIP: See it during snowmelt

DON'T MISS: The big pines

CREATURE FEATURE: Brown creeper

TREASURE HUNT: The iron buttons on the railroad ties

FAVORITE MONTH: April

SNAPSHOT: The falls with Bennington behind them

OWNERSHIP: Town of Bennington; managed by the Bennington Conservation Commission

DIRECTIONS:

Learning to Observe

There is an art to taking a mindful meander. Walks have different purposes at different times. Sometimes you need an adventure, other times a therapy session, or perhaps you're looking to experience awe and wonder.

Go beyond the visual and receive all that nature is offering through your senses, allowing its full spectrum to reach you.

Let curiosity lead. Consider letting your eyes and ears guide you—following a bird or away from the hum of a mower, following a waterway, heading to a patch of light. Lean into the gifts of the changing seasons. On unseasonably warm days, follow the sun. Embrace the winter by grabbing a pair of snowshoes for the journey. Swim or bike in the summer. Notice the little things up close, and stop to appreciate the distant spaces where few humans will ever set foot. Be there to experience the special moments within each season and the rhythms of each day.

Nature saves her best secrets for those who take their time. Shelve the agenda of reaching the summit and give your eyes permission to hunt for magic: a morning spiderweb catching light like spun glass, a knotted tree twisting into an ancient creature, or a nest of birds hidden in plain sight.

Top right photo by Chuck Carlson

How do we observe the world around us? No matter how small the journey is, there may be something new to see, hear, smell, touch, and feel. Go into airplane mode, both on your phone and in the sense of becoming an observer on a journey.

Spread your wings! Go solo, or explore with a friend. Take an active role in learning by journaling, sketching, or photographing your observations.

Clear any expectations of what the outcomes may be; seek answers or messages, or clarity, but don't expect them. You may have to listen for a long time. It takes patience to learn the language of nature, and sometimes longer to interpret what it has to say. But if you make a practice of observing the rhythms of the natural world, meaningful encounters abound. To go out for the sunset, for instance, to track its progress as it drops over ridge, valley, or water, is a particular gift. In such a spectacular landscape, this seemingly ordinary part of the day becomes a great wonder. To see a familiar thing newly feels like a revelation.

I go to Nature to be soothed and healed, and to have my senses put in tune.

—*John Burroughs*

BEECH HILL
FINDING MICROS

2

Restful Vista
Dublin

Walk Summary

Rising steeply above the high-elevation village of Dublin, Beech Hill offers one of the closest and finest vantage points of Grand Monadnock. But you'll have to search for small pocket views tucked away on the several miles of spruce- and oak-covered trails. Along the way, Beech Hill features a gentle meander through a meadow, connection to a healing past, and an invitation to mountain trails for hiking.

Highlights

- Sit in the "stone throne" looking out to the east
- Slowly take in the sights, sounds, and smells along the accessible Meadow Trail
- Feel a sense of renewal guided by a restored landscape
- Search for hidden Monadnock views that lie beyond the loop
- In summer, feel the warm breeze roll across a hilltop meadow

From town, the approach winds up a steep mountain road beside the Dublin School, a private preparatory school. Midway up the hill, on its eastern slope, is a parking area and kiosk. From here, several trails unfurl—some well established and others still evolving. This is a trail system that invites you to explore it piece by piece.

Beech Hill Farm opened as an addiction treatment center in 1949, which were just beginning to emerge in the United States. Its model of rehabilitation through farmwork was pioneering. The facility grew in the 1970s and '80s into a one-hundred-bed operation, treating thousands, including the occasional celebrity. On winter nights, the large buildings were ablaze with lights, and this bright outpost was dubbed the "city on the hill." But by 2001, after a period of controversy and decline, it closed. For years afterward, the shuttered buildings stood stark on the hillside.

A Vision of Conservation and Stewardship

Eventually, the buildings were removed, and a vision for ecological and community restoration began to take root. In 2005, the Beech Hill–Dublin Lake Watershed Association formed to protect both the land and the lake below. Partnering with the Monadnock Conservancy, they purchased the sixty-three-acre Beech Hill property and established the first of two permanent conservation easements in 2008. Restoration followed. The old septic lagoon was filled, and meadows were reclaimed. Hidden remnants of the site now remain, a water tower being perhaps the most notable. Like recovery itself, the transformation is still a work in progress.

Beech Hill sits at a watershed divide, feeding both the Merrimack and Connecticut River systems, and plays a major role in keeping Dublin Lake clean and clear. Its forest is a mix of red oak, birch, maple, spruce, and beech. Some pockets have remained uncut for decades, offering an increasingly rare glimpse of older New England forest.

Paths to Discovery

In 2010, forester Swift Corwin designed a trail system here: the Zig Zag and Ridge Trails. The Old Carriage Road, built in the 1920s, climbs to Eagle Rock, a prominent rocky outcrop, where a south-facing view of Monadnock awaits. To the north, you can see Skatutakee and Thumb Mountains in the foreground, as well as distant wind turbines and Mount Kearsarge. A nice short loop returns via the Ridge Trail, but longer extensions are possible.

The SuperSanctuary's newest universal access trail is a resource for all.

From the hilltop, near the cell tower, is the new all-persons Meadow Trail, which loops through the restored meadow and woods. The trail, built in 2025, is a welcome addition that promises greater accessibility for all who seek nature's calm and inspiration. About a third of a mile in total, which includes a lollipop loop, it traverses the meadow and provides sitting areas and eastern views. Don't miss a chance to sit in the natural "stone chair" set in a large boulder and facing Crotched Mountain. Take three deep breaths while sitting here, and notice how you feel.

Red oak trees may be the real stars of Beech Hill. They dominate the hillsides, their leaves, nectar, and acorns providing an important food source to numerous caterpillars, insects, birds, and mammals. At higher elevations like Beech Hill, red oaks grow alongside red spruce (bottom left), a pairing that is not common outside the Monadnock Region.

The east-facing view reveals the Belknap Mountains and Pawtuckaways, with Crotched Mountain prominent at the center. A set of benches and rocks invites you to rest and reflect here, perhaps while watching hawks fly overhead or listening to insects hum.

The hilltop meadow, which changes with the seasons, is a restoration work in progress; the goal is to attract bees, butterflies, and a diversity of birds and other wildlife. In winter, search for tracks of foxes and deer, which crisscross the snow. A southerly breeze often cuts through and provides welcome cooling on hot summer days.

By midsummer, the meadow teems with invertebrates, including dragonflies and butterflies. Here, a calico pennant adds a flash of vibrant red.

Photo by Kate McKay

Notice the oaks, which are more prevalent in Beech Hill's canopy, ironically, than its namesake tree. They leaf out late in May, when the warblers come through, and turn amber by late October. Their stark, barren beauty in winter is equally compelling. The beeches are fading quickly due to the invasive beech leaf disease, an ecological shift being monitored across the region. One has to wonder if, like Beech Hill Farm, beech trees might also be relics of the past.

Farther on is the South Outlook, a quiet gem tucked into the woods, which offers a spectacular pocket view of Monadnock rising over Dublin Lake, a patchwork of colors and textures. Like this trail's other viewpoints, it's not marked with fanfare, but you'll be able to navigate there. Another new trail is the steeper Lake Trail, which winds half a mile between the lake and the meadow, accessed across the driveway from the start of the Meadow Trail, behind the cell towers.

Beech Hill's still-evolving trail system invites you to explore and linger at its viewpoints, immerse yourself in its history, and restore yourself by taking it all in. Walk its trails in comfort and with openness. Venture farther into its vast trail system if you're so inclined. Its past is visible in its historical relics, its presence is shaped by a vibrant community of stewards, and its future is one of healing in nature for all who visit.

One of Beech Hill's many viewpoints.

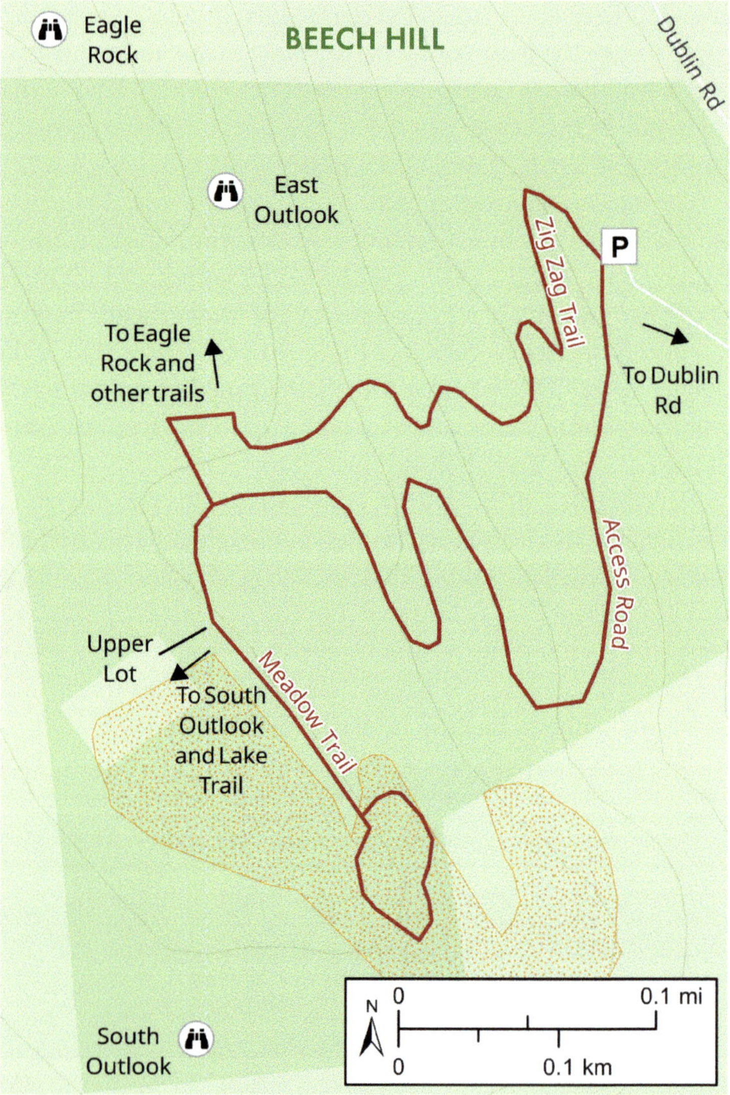

Check https://www.monadnockconservancy.org/explore/hiking for more details.

Lay of the Land

TRAILS: 0.3-mile Meadow Trail meets accessibility standards; several miles of other trails, including Zig Zag, Eagle Rock, Ridge, and Lake Trails, with varied terrain

ACCESS: From Dublin town center, take Dublin Road toward Harrisville. After you pass the Dublin School and William North Road, look for Beech Hill Road soon on the left. Take this dirt road and park in the mid-level parking lot; a gate provides access to the all-persons Meadow Trail and an upper parking area. Gate access is limited, so expect to walk the half-mile paved stretch to the Meadow Trail.

PERMITTED USES: See the Monadnock Conservancy website for all regulations

A GREAT PLACE TO: Explore comfortably in a hilltop meadow

INSIDER TIP: Join a local organization's field trip for parking access to the all-persons trail

DON'T MISS: The "stone throne"

CREATURE FEATURE: Autumn meadowhawk

TREASURE HUNT: The old water tower

FAVORITE MONTH: June

SNAPSHOT: Monadnock view from South Outlook

OWNERSHIP: Beech Hill–Dublin Lake Watershed Association

DIRECTIONS:

MicroExploring Practices

Finding Micros

MicroExploring is a personal call to curiosity and wonder. Every path is a small adventure, and every trail has a gift for you that can be as simple as peace, perspective, clarity, or an observation that sparks inspiration.

We like to think that we know the area we live in pretty well. MicroExploring challenges this notion by making us curious about the blind spots in our home geography. What's behind this hill? Where does this stream originate and flow out to? What's beyond this dead-end road? MicroExploring invites you to slow down, pay attention, and appreciate the beauty and wonder that exists just beyond your doorstep. Discovering the world right around you is a grounding, healing, and powerful action.

Discovering the Overlooked

Explore your neighborhood by choosing roads you usually ignore and consider alternating how you explore them. A road you usually take by car will be completely different by bike or on foot. Your neighbors and friends are likely to be stashing a secret walk or two, so make sure to regularly ask the people in your network where they like to explore. Local hiking guides and maps are always a good start, but keep in mind that many other trails and roads are open to the public, perhaps not sign-posted or clearly marked.

Make a habit of picking up tidbits of knowledge about the natural history along trails. Many trails offer this information at their starting point. Open your mind and feed your curiosity; do a quick dive into the local geology or history; consider one of the wildlife residents, trees, or plants that calls your attention. The more you know, the more you will appreciate and the more you will receive.

Trusting the Road

Getting lost on purpose can be a surprisingly beautiful way to discover what's been hiding in plain sight. Sometimes we'll just get in the car with no plan, taking turns choosing left, right, or straight—letting instinct and landscape decide. It's part game, part philosophy; loosen the grip, trust the road. When you stop trying to control the destination, you often end up exactly where you needed to be.

Mapping Your Treasures

Keeping track of interesting trails or locations can be tricky, but Google Maps can serve as a kind of external memory. When you stumble upon a trailhead, viewpoint, or landmark that catches your eye, drop a pin and save it to a list. These saved spots can create a simple visual system: green for places to explore, hearts for favorites. Over time, this turns the map into a living guide—easy to check, easy to follow, and always ready with inspiration for the next MicroExploration. Other useful apps are on XBackcountry, AllTrails, or Gaia GPS. These apps' highly detailed maps allow you to see aerial views and identify places you might want to visit, like bodies of water, streams, hills, or rock formations.

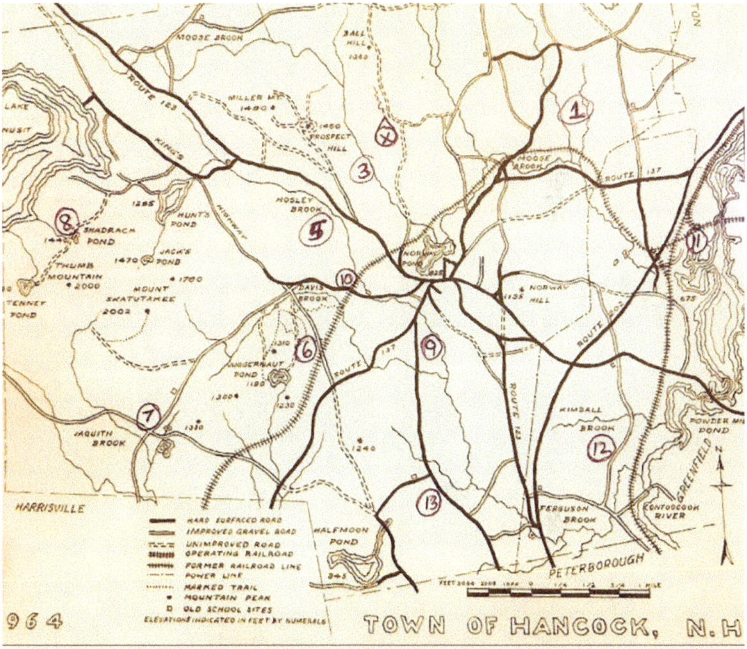

This old map is how MicroExploring started for us, as we began marking down all the wonders near our homes. Through that process, we unlocked the powerful truth that adventure isn't about mileage but rather depth. Our own backyards became new universes to explore.

MicroExploring is, in a way, like building a personal collection of hyperlocal experiences. Each hidden trail, viewpoint, or stream becomes part of a personal stash. Once this mindset takes hold, you'll likely find your perception shifting. Soon, almost without conscious thought, whether you're driving familiar roads or walking a new path, your eyes will constantly scan your surroundings. You'll instinctively seek out potential starting points for your next adventure: an intriguing gap in an old stone wall, an unpaved track veering into the woods, an inviting glimpse of water. The quiet hunt for the next gem becomes a constant background hum of curiosity and delight.

ELMWOOD JUNCTION
BIRDING BASICS

3

Cove-Side Crossroads

Hancock

The earth has music for
those who listen.

—George Santayana

Walk Summary

An easy, flat approach from which to experience railroad history and witness phenomenal bird migrations, the Elmwood Junction trails follow old railroad grades and traverse a variety of habitats. Lovers of turtles, snakes, birds, and dragonflies will find delight here in spring and summer, and in winter, skiers and snowshoers can enjoy the solitude of these trails just off the beaten path.

Highlights

- Step back into the past and envision a busy railroad depot
- Watch for migrations of waterfowl, warblers, and nighthawks
- Search for snakes, turtles, and their nests, as well as mammal scat, along the tracks
- Follow the sun to cove views or take cover under the shade of wooded trails
- Paddle Powder Mill Pond to witness eagles, otters, and turtles up close

This adventure begins at the wooden bridge on Robinson Road in Hancock, just seconds from busy Route 202. The transition is instant and drastic, from asphalt and traffic to birdsong and quiet water. Once a bustling depot, Elmwood Junction was the crossroads of the Manchester & Keene and Peterborough & Hillsborough Railroads. For several decades, northbound vacationers shared tracks with southbound shipments of milk and eggs. But when the trains stopped, forests grew back and beavers returned, building dams. This once-bustling junction of tracks near the confluence of the Contoocook River and Moose Brook is now a haven for wildlife and a welcome respite for locals.

Elmwood Junction is a haven for wildlife, including river otters (top), milk snakes (bottom left), and snapping turtle hatchlings (bottom right).

Top photo by Chuck Carlson

Elmwood Junction was conserved thanks to a joint effort by the Harris Center and the Town of Hancock, with the land sold at just $10,000 by Dick Amidon, a long-serving Hancock selectperson. This small sum purchased a forever value for wildlife and historical preservation, as well as for recreation.

Park at either of the open places on either side of the gate. The house ahead, the former Robinson House, is privately owned, so please observe it from a distance. It's the site of the second Hancock post office between 1880 and 1933. Before the railroad, this was a quiet farm growing potatoes, beets, milk, and hay. By the late nineteenth century, it had transformed into a summer retreat for city visitors, with a promise of fresh air and restoration.

In a short period of time, the area's landscape has been altered by the construction of railroads, the damming of waterways, and the clearing of land and diversion of wetlands for agriculture, but a wild mosaic of forests and wetlands has returned and thrives today.
Photo by Meade Cadot

Start your walk at the interpretive panel near the parking areas on the left end of Robinson Road. This panel, along with several others along the trails, is the result of a recent Eagle Scout project supported by the Harris Center and the Hancock Conservation Commission. The placards, complete with period photos, are a wealth of information about the various structures that once stood in this small, temporary village. As you stop to read, try to imagine the train whistle across the pastures, cattle and sheep in the fields, vacationers in formal attire. How far could one see across the landscape?

The Confluence to the Junction

Across Robinson Road, Moose Brook spills into Powder Mill Pond, forming a marshy cove. The pond represents a portion of the Contoocook that was dammed for the production of gunpowder around two hundred years ago. Scan the pond here and admire the granite buttresses, which once supported a railroad bridge. Today, rough-winged swallows nest in the granite blocks where a small elm sprouts, and the pond is a reliable spot to watch for turtles, otters, and marsh birds. Waterfowl congregate in the cove in spring and fall, and bald eagles stir them up periodically. Turn and walk alongside the brook's entrance to explore a sandy bank where turtles haul themselves out to nest. From here, savor a good view of the marsh where birds flit and feed and beavers can sometimes be seen. The bank is a good place to get some sunlight before heading into the wooded trails.

Back across the road, a narrow path leads along an old railroad corridor. Note the large vernal pool on your right before the trail narrows through brushy vegetation, which may contain some ticks and poison ivy. If you wish to avoid those hazards, stick to the main rail trail starting at the kiosk, which is wider and less vegetated. But if you follow the narrower trail system, which approaches the sound of Route 202, you'll reach a small grove of aspens where another trail merges with this one. Continue at the bend, away from the noise on its other leg and observe the altered landforms, likely the result of railroad track construction in the 1870s.

After passing pine and aspen forests, you'll see another sign. Straight ahead is a wide trail parallel to the main rail trail, which we often reserve for the return trip. A direct out-and-back to Powder Mill Pond and the old railroad bridge is reached by a right turn followed by a quick left onto a wide dirt road. Some deeper ruts in this road may contain puddles and be prohibitive for wheelchairs and strollers. Shady hemlocks provide cover up to the small bridge over a wetland. Sandy patches and sunlit logs make great basking spots for turtles, and the wild cove on the right frames a distant view of Pack Monadnock. The bend ahead, which impounds, or encloses, an expansive wetland, is known as Magoon's Curve.

Following the Tracks

Stay right at the tracks onto the old Hillsborough line to enjoy a long, straight stretch with good visibility and sun. Walk along a narrow corridor to the right of the tracks that is firm and just wide enough. This is one of our favorite places to let the mind wander and disconnect. A morning or evening walk here keeps you out of the hot midday sun baking down on the railroad grade.

The trains have stopped running, but the tracks remain. Follow this human pathway, either with company or in solitude.

As the south end of Powder Mill Pond appears on the right, a productive vernal pool can be seen on the left (and sometimes heard—listen for duck-like calls of wood frogs in spring). A rusty metal railroad bridge, tagged with colorful graffiti, spans the narrowest point of Powder Mill Pond. From here, you can see the pond's linear, north-south orientation, hinting at its true origins; in fact, the pond is a section of the dammed Contoocook River. Scan for waterfowl on the pond and for ospreys, bald eagles, and belted kingfishers in nearby trees or flying by. Birders often observe huge nighthawk migrations along the shores of Powder Mill Pond in late August, so watch the sky, too.

Loop back via the bend at Magoon's Curve, then take a sharp left onto a grassy, sometimes wet path. In high tick season or during wasp activity, you might prefer the main corridor instead. The tracks are a great place to find mammal scat left by coyotes or foxes, and sometimes turtles trapped between the rails. Either way, you'll return to the parking area with a new understanding of the land and probably a few birds added to your list. For a longer point-to-point walk, continue past the railroad bridge to the Cilley Family Forest in Greenfield, where the journey continues. However you come and go, make sure to bring binoculars and a sense of wonder!

Visitors can walk, boat, bike, or ski to the old railroad bridge, where they can observe migrating birds and enjoy the water views.

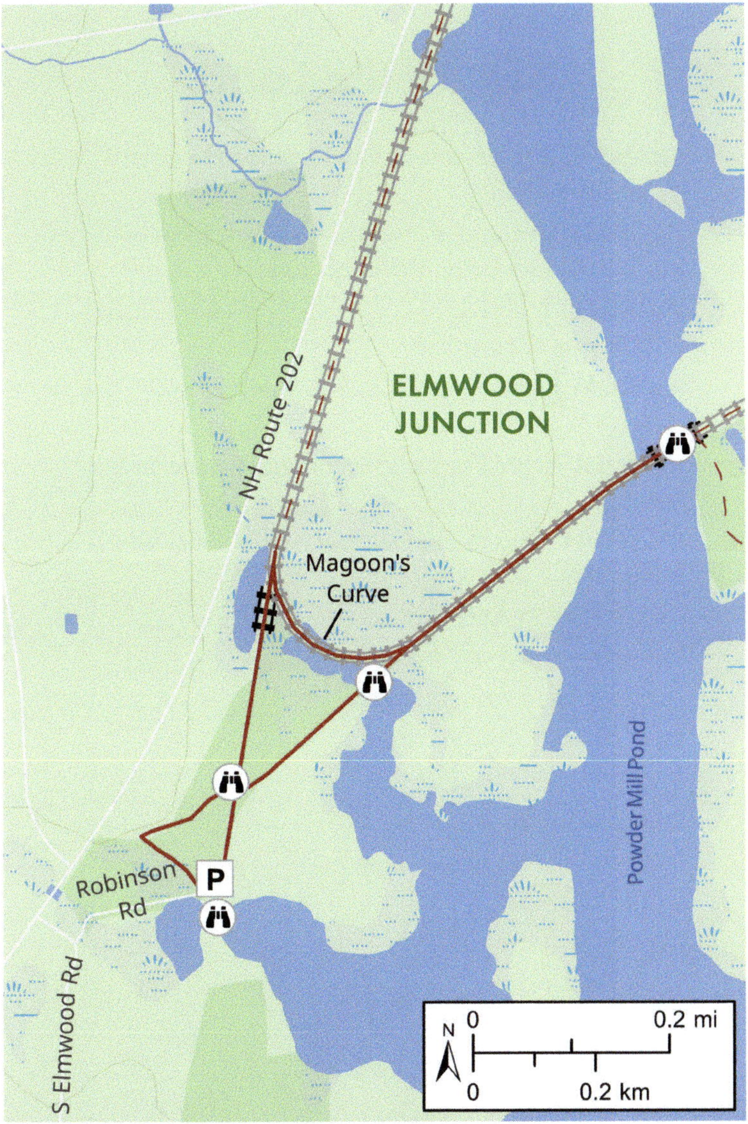
ELMWOOD JUNCTION
NH Route 202
Magoon's Curve
Powder Mill Pond
Robinson Rd
S Elmwood Rd
P
N
0
0.2 mi
0
0.2 km

Lay of the Land

TRAILS: One mile of unmarked but open trails on mainly level ground

ACCESS: Parking at the end of Robinson Road off Route 202 near South Elmwood Road

PERMITTED USES: No motorized vehicles; hunting permitted in season

A GREAT PLACE TO: Observe waterfowl and warbler migrations

INSIDER TIP: Visit on a spring morning or summer evening

DON'T MISS: The peaceful vistas from the railroad bridge

CREATURE FEATURE: Common nighthawk

TREASURE HUNT: The huge trunk of a snapped cottonwood tree along the main trail by the old station

FAVORITE MONTH: May

SNAPSHOT: Moose Brook rail abutment

OWNERSHIP: Town of Hancock; managed by the Hancock Conservation Commission

DIRECTIONS:

MicroExploring Practices

Birding Basics

Birding has steadily gained popularity, especially since the pandemic. It has benefits on so many levels, especially when we make a regular practice of it. Birding helps us focus, improves our memories, and enhances mental and physical health. It brings us joy, peace, and connection—both to the natural world and, often, to other humans. And learning about particular creatures leads easily to wanting to protect them and their habitats. Birds can be a gateway to learning about other taxa, too—butterflies, dragonflies, trees, and so on. Best of all, you don't need any special knowledge to begin: anyone can be a birder.

As we've come to define MicroExploring, we've realized how essential observing birds is to this practice. Looking for birds forces your mind to shift from your inner self to your environment. Your senses begin to sharpen; at the same time, they become wider and more receptive. Finding a bright scarlet tanager or American goldfinch is a treat for the eyes; learning their songs reveals unexpected presences sharing space with you, hidden in the trees, marshes, or fields. As you come to know a place through repeated visits, you'll start to notice patterns of bird distribution and behavior, giving a new perspective to your walk every time.

The SuperSanctuary is blessed with an abundance of incredible birds. In any given year, as many as two hundred species can be found within its boundaries, and nearly half raise young

Even seeing the world in black and white can be striking: black-and-white warblers are one of two dozen warbler species that pass through the SuperSanctuary during migration.

Photo by Chuck Carlson

here. Bald eagles and common loons breed on several of its larger lakes and ponds. Colorful warblers sing, woodpeckers drum, and owls call throughout its vast woodlands, while hawks soar over its spruce forests atop the wild ridgelines. But even in urban settings, such as downtown Peterborough, you'll discover a wealth of birds, too. They stitch together our different landscapes into a whole. Though particular birds change with the seasons and with the landscape, they are our constant companions.

Birding is for everyone, and birds are an omnipresent form of wildlife. It's only human to want to connect with them!

Right photo by Ben Conant

What You Need

Curiosity, a field guide, and a decent pair of binoculars are all you need to get started, but there are other ways to enjoy and learn birds. The Merlin Bird ID app is a particularly useful tool for learning bird songs, and many people record their observations in the eBird app, which also allows them to contribute to citizen-science efforts to monitor birds. Sketching, photography, and journaling bring enhanced cognition and health benefits.

Setting some goals (such as learning about one new bird each month) will make the journey seem more manageable.

Birding can be done alone or with others, and growth will occur by doing a little of both. No matter your level of experience, consider joining an expert-led field trip with The Harris Center, the Monadnock Bird and Nature Club, or another local group.

One way to enjoy birds is by designating a "sit spot"—an intentional practice of being still and observing birds around you. Watch their behavior, listen to vocalizations and interactions. When your feet are planted and you are still, you may notice more.

All you need to get started learning about and appreciating birds is curiosity, a field guide, and a pair of binoculars. You can join an expert-led field trip with the Harris Center or the Monadnock Bird and Nature Club.

Photo by Ben Conant

Birding by the Seasons

Winter may be a slow time for bird diversity, as many species have left the Northeast for warmer places, but it's an excellent time to connect with the fewer species present, study their behaviors, and truly learn them. Spring is heralded as the most exciting time for birding in the SuperSanctuary, when—with some effort and a solid knowledge of bird identification and habitats—upward of one hundred species of breeding and migratory birds can be found on a given day. Many are in full song, and they can easily be seen before the trees leaf out in late May.

Summer features abundant birdsong through mid-July, but birds are generally harder to see in leafy wooded habitats. Try birding by ear or searching for them by boat during this time. In the fall, many species are on the move again, and migration tends to extend longer. Some species have less coloration due to molting, and there's a lot less song, but bird concentrations can be rather impressive, and it's a great time to find unusual species, or "rarities"—an exciting prospect for many birders.

Birding Hot Spots in the SuperSanctuary

Conservation groups and private landowners alike have long prioritized stewardship actions for birds. While the birding can be thrilling nearly everywhere in the SuperSanctuary, well-known places to observe birds include Elmwood Junction, Loverens Mill Cedar Swamp, Pitcher Mountain, Robb Reservoir, Willard Pond, Crotched Mountain, the Hiroshi Loop Trail, and the Pack Monadnock Raptor Observatory at Miller State Park.

Additional Resources

- American Birding Association Code of Ethics: https://www.aba.org/aba-code-of-birding-ethics
- eBird: https://www.eBird.org
- Joy of Birding: https://www.joyofbirding.nhaudubon.org
- Merlin Bird ID app: https://www.merlin.allaboutbirds.org
- Monadnock Bird and Nature Club: https://www.monadnockbirdclub.wixsite.com/mbnc

A watchful eye will yield treasures such as this barred owl peering through the foliage.

CROTCHED MOUNTAIN 4
THE MEDICINE OF MOVEMENT

Accessible Ascent

Greenfield, Bennington, and Francestown

The mountains are the
high altars of the earth.

—John Ruskin

Walk Summary

Crotched Mountain is a place with a rich history of healing and innovation; its universal-access trails are built with care and integrate beautifully with their natural surroundings. They offer options to explore a meadow, a marsh, and several forest types, along with intriguing evidence of the area's past. A viewpoint offers the chance for spectacular scenery and a glimpse of seasonal raptor migration.

Highlights

- View the SuperSanctuary from beyond its borders on Blueberry Ridge
- Taste the ancestral berries from the first cultivated highbush blueberries
- Tap into your sense of history as you find traces of an old sugar bush operation
- Move along a trail system designed with comfort and beauty for all
- Scan the skies in the fall for migrating broad-winged hawks and other raptors

Atop a prominent isolated hilltop where three towns' lines meet is a place rich in firsts: the site of early historical achievements in rehabilitation, agriculture, and wind power. Crotched Mountain, a sprawling, low mountain recognizable from nearly every part of the SuperSanctuary, can claim an even more notable distinction: the longest mountainside accessible trail system in the country. Created by renowned trail designer Peter Jensen, the accessible trail system here opened in 2011; it was built to US Forest Service accessibility standards and remains a model for inclusive outdoor design. Stewarded by longtime caretaker Rick Fife, with help from dedicated volunteer groups, the trails are open, safe, and welcoming.

Park in the large lot and make your way to the trailhead, where a set of interpretive signs tells the story of the land and the trail's design. A sweeping view of meadow and mountain greets you. Depending on your mood, choose one of two trails.

MicroExploring doesn't need to be contained by a boundary.

Gregg Trail to Blueberry Ridge (0.8 miles)

This shorter trail ascends through a meadow and young forest to Blueberry Ridge. It returns to a clearing, where you will experience fabulous panoramic views of the surrounding hills and valleys.

Take the left fork at the trailhead to begin your ascent along a gentle slope through an open meadow, inviting an easy meander and side-by-side walking on the hard-packed trail. The meadow is full of colorful wildflowers that bloom in summer and fall and are carefully managed to encourage pollinators and other invertebrates. The milkweed can be spectacular some years and is an important food source for migratory monarch butterflies. Fragrant sweetfern, a small shrub in the wax-myrtle family, grows atop this rise. Crush up and smell one of its long, narrow leaves to reap the full sensory benefits of a summer hike here.

From the meadow, a panoramic eastern view opens up across lowlands toward Manchester, tracing the contours of the Uncanoonucs, Joe English Hill, Winn Mountain, and Rose Mountain, far to the east of the SuperSanctuary's boundary. An interpretive sign helps you identify the summits. This view shows that MicroExploring doesn't need to be contained within a boundary.

The trail soon enters a young forest, taking a sinuous and gradual route uphill, passing multi-trunked (coppiced) red maples and white pines regenerated from an old field. Notice the smaller stature of the trees in this forest and the high density of trunks compared to an older one with larger, well-spaced trees. The forest here once supported blueberry production, shaded shrubs now the only evidence of the area's botanical history. Frederick Coville, pioneer of the commercial highbush blueberry, conducted his work nearby in Greenfield beginning in 1905. He crossed particularly flavorful highbush and lowbush blueberry plants from his neighbors' properties, which led to the foundation of the commercial highbush blueberry. Wild lowbush and highbush blueberries, the offspring of Coville's plantings on Crotched Mountain, still line the trail in places, ripe for tasting in late July.

Stone walls emerge, remnants of sheep-pasturing days. A lush understory of ferns, shrubs, and herbaceous plants fills in beneath young hardwoods. It's a choice spot to walk on a blustery spring day when one might be reluctant to venture underneath big trees, and there's enough shade in summer to stay cool. Smooth boulders dot the edge of this trail in many places and allow for safe scrambling. Whether you're walking with mobility aids, exploring with young kids, or just looking for a different trail experience, this is one of the most accessible and least tick-prone trails you'll find.

The cultivation of highbush blueberries has its roots on these slopes.

As the trail enters a younger forest, look for lowbush blueberries in July and blackberries in August. Summer's sweet smell of hay-scented fern is in the air, and juniper also grows along the trail's edge, its berries reminiscent of gin when pinched. This evergreen ground cover grows best on eroded soils, indicative of the sheep-grazing history of this region well over a century ago. From a hexagonal viewing platform, you can see North Pack, Pack Monadnock, Mount Monadnock, and other Super-Sanctuary summits, as well as Powder Mill Pond. This vantage is a prime location to watch soaring hawks, glimpse the dipping sun, and admire changing weather and clouds. If you're lucky, a visit in mid-September may reveal the spectacle of hundreds or more broad-winged hawks in a day!

Terrestrial wildlife also thrives here—look for basking garter and smooth green snakes, young forest songbirds like eastern towhees and chestnut-sided warblers, dragonflies, butterflies, and other insects foraging on the diverse plant life. In winter, the view remains excellent, with the changing snow and light conditions. Bring water and sun protection if you plan to linger at the top, as it's open and exposed.

In mid-September, you may be rewarded with the sighting of a broad-winged hawk or even an entire "kettle" of hawks.

Photo by Chuck Carlson

This trail demonstrates that one doesn't always need to get to the summit to enjoy the best view. Crotched's pinnacle, farther up and reachable via a longer trail, is wooded and closed in. Here on Blueberry Ridge, both the view and the blueberries are the reward. For a faster descent, a grassy shortcut trail parallels the Gregg Trail. It doesn't meet accessibility standards and may have ticks, but it's a quick route back down.

Dutton Brook Trail (2.0 miles round trip)

This longer, shaded trail descends into a former beaver swamp, now regenerating as a young forest, and winds beautifully around its perimeter, featuring diverse tree species, observation areas, and boardwalks.

Starting down the trail, watch for the pocket view, which showcases Crotched Mountain's expansive, multi-topped summit over the sloping meadow. Notice strips of dark green (red spruce and taller white pines) that interrupt the hardwoods. The summit is still recovering from its time as the world's first commercial wind farm. Built in 1980, this twenty-turbine facility featured towers just sixty feet tall. Though once considered a failure here, the venture led directly to the development of the modern wind-power industry.

Pass a stone wall near some larger trees, and pause to enter a small grove of sugar maples on the right. These open-grown, irregularly shaped trees were formerly part of a sugar bush operation, producing maple syrup. Look for occasional old tap holes (small, healed-over circles) at chest height, and for rows of neat tap holes made by the yellow-bellied sapsucker. Feel the tough, platy bark of these older trees, a tactile connection to the past.

A gentle path leads the eye and allows for safe and easy exploration by people of all ages and abilities.

This trail was carefully constructed with attention to detail. It encourages mindfulness as its stable footing allows you to raise your eyes and awareness. The trail widens out beautifully for long stretches, too, so members of your party can hike together side by side.

Continue along the stone walls that cross diagonally. Look for larger red oak and yellow birch trees that grow along the wall. These were landmarks that also served as fence posts and shade trees. At the loop, we usually choose to circle this trail clockwise, but it could be done in the other direction. Notice how yellow and black birches often establish on rotting stumps. As the stumps rot away, gaps between the trunk and the ground are exposed through the new trees' leggy roots.

Make more discoveries by moving slowly and intentionally, letting your senses take in interesting shapes. By letting your curiosity lead, you may add knowledge to your discoveries, such as the reason a birch tree might grow leggy roots.

The trail conceals a wetland feature on the right. A viewing platform showcases regenerating shrubs and saplings growing in a former beaver swamp, but don't expect a water view. The beaver pond has long ago developed into a meadow following beaver abandonment, and now this meadow has given way to a young forest. Songbirds like common yellowthroats and red-winged blackbirds can be observed here if you sit quietly. It's a good place for a stretch.

A short boardwalk section winds through wet ground. Its recycled plastic planks have warped over time and are moss-covered but remain strong. Search for the stream's outlet where a stone wall crosses the brook on the right, where a single stone lies perched above the outlet of the brook. Perhaps the stone was placed long ago, perhaps more recently. No doubt this wall helped the beavers dam a former pond, the evidence towering above in the form of dead pines. The trail returns and ascends gently toward a twisted, hollowed maple where the loop completes.

Ruby-throated hummingbird painting in Francestown by Rosemary Conroy.

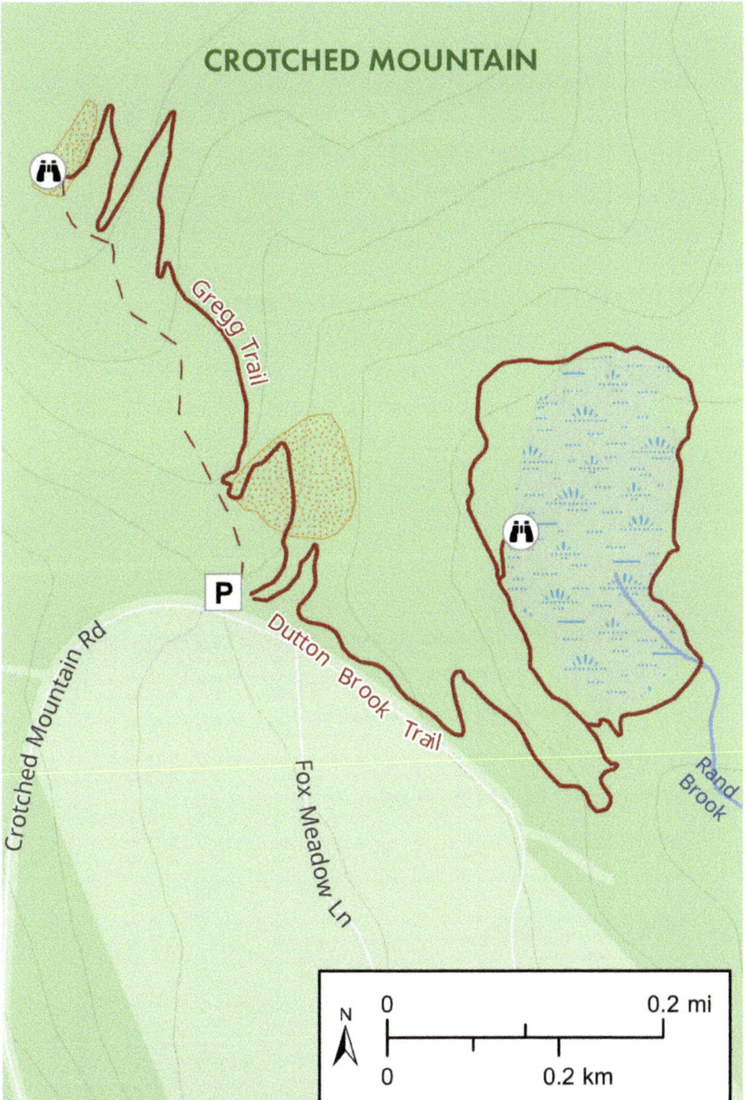
CROTCHED MOUNTAIN
Gregg Trail
P
Dutton Brook Trail
Crotched Mountain Rd
Fox Meadow Ln
Rand Brook
N
0
0.2 mi
0
0.2 km

Lay of the Land

TRAILS: 2.8 miles (round trip) of universally accessible, hard-packed gravel trails with some elevation gain

ACCESS: Parking area near the end of Crotched Mountain Road in Greenfield; on the left past Verney Drive

PERMITTED USES: No motorized vehicles or bikes (motorized and manual wheelchairs are allowed); service animals only; open from 30 minutes after sunrise until 30 minutes before sunset; trails closed during mud season and excessively wet times

A GREAT PLACE TO: Discover a mountainside accessible trail

INSIDER TIP: Go early or late to see how light reflects off the landscape

DON'T MISS: The platform on Blueberry Ridge

CREATURE FEATURE: Broad-winged hawk

TREASURE HUNT: Tap holes in the sugar maple grove just off the trail

FAVORITE MONTH: October

SNAPSHOT: View from Gregg Trail platform

OWNERSHIP: Crotched Mountain Foundation

DIRECTIONS:

MicroExploring Practices

The Medicine of Movement

Across every culture, on every continent, humans dance. People move to grieve, to celebrate, to call the rain. Dance is older than agriculture, older than the drum, maybe older than speech. It's one of the few things all humans do and have always done. Movement is one of our original ways of processing, expressing, and connecting, but in daily life, most of us barely move. We sit. We scroll. We store tension. We forget that we're made to sway with the wind, to bend with the landscape, to breathe like part of the weather.

Break free from the rigidity of what being an adult means. Allow your body to express itself against the backdrop of nature's palette.

Waking the Body

We always begin our MicroExploring group walks with a bit of movement. Even a few minutes of warm-up exercises set us up for success. On their own, a lot of people skip this part: they feel that without a "professional" leading them, they don't know what to do. That could not be further from the truth. You don't need to be a yoga or tai chi instructor to practice the art of movement—your body knows, and learning to listen to it, giving it what it needs, is just as important as the actual trek in nature.

Any type of mindful movement—whether it's yoga, tai chi, or simple stretching—affects us more powerfully if done outdoors because there's nothing between us, the sky, and the earth.

The goal of movement is to connect not just to nature but also to yourself. Begin by focusing on your breath and feeling the ground. Your body is not separate from nature; it's nature remembering itself. Invite movement. Your joints, muscles, and bones know what they need. This isn't about cardio; it's about arrival. Go toward slight discomfort and anything that needs stretching. Simply raising your hands above your head and stretching is a great place to start. Once there, you can scan your body and begin moving your arms, neck, and legs in circles. You might hear crackling and noises like wires in the rusty parts of the human machine. Follow them.

Flowing Freely

There's no right or wrong way to go from here. Let your body improvise. Let it remember the shapes it enjoyed, the rhythms that felt natural. You don't need to follow a strict form. Mixing elements from practices like yoga, tai chi, or qigong into your own flow is powerful. This kind of intuitive stretching and slow movement—done on your own terms—builds both confidence and connection. The more you practice, the more your body will want to return to it. Nature becomes your studio, and your own breath becomes the guide.

A personal movement routine tells your body that you're listening to it. You don't need a guru or trainer. Just allow your body to tell you what needs attention and enjoy moving with freedom outside.

Photo by Ben Conant

The walk to take to-day is the walk you took yesterday.

—John Burroughs

EASTVIEW RAIL TRAIL
WHEELS AND WANDERINGS 5

Hidden Passage
Harrisville

Photo by Brett Amy Thelen

Walk Summary

Rail trails are one of the region's best-kept secrets, and when you walk, ski, or bike them, history, along with nature, unfolds before you. The Eastview Rail Trail follows a historic rail route through wildlife-rich forests and wetlands in a town defined by a vibrant textiles tradition that continues today. Hike point-to-point one way, or make a bigger trip of it.

Highlights

- Connect the conserved landscapes of the SuperSanctuary by rail trail
- Ponder the history of railroads and "sheep fever" in Historic Harrisville
- Take an easygoing shaded saunter to a wildlife-rich beaver pond
- Admire the undulating landscape and our efforts to tame it
- Try this trail by bike or on cross-country skis
- Enjoy the culinary delights of the Harrisville General Store as a treat

The Eastview Rail Trail, at just a mile and a half long, connects two scenic parts of Harrisville, a picturesque historic village famous for its textile mills. Though Harrisville was one of the last towns incorporated in the region, the railroad's opening in 1878 quickly put it on the map. The Manchester & Keene line spurred growth in textile mills as new markets opened up in cities. And to supply the mills with fleece, "sheep fever" took over New England, with thousands of acres cleared for raising sheep, particularly Merinos, prized for their dense coats. Here and elsewhere, the region abounds with reminders of this era: stone walls crisscross the landscape, and there's even a granite "sheep tunnel" under the railroad near its western terminus on Hancock Road.

Bike, walk, or ski the Eastview Rail Trail, depending upon the season, and discover something new each time.

Begin at the small parking area on Jaquith Road in the former hamlet of Eastview, which hosted a railroad station and mill at one time. Park in the little lot by the gate, and set foot on the rail trail, which is flat, even, and immediately remote. As you walk, imagine the effort it took to build a railroad through this terrain. Mountains were literally moved to build it: granite was blasted, trestles constructed, wetlands ditched and diverted, and earth piled in order to lay tracks. Harrisville was chosen as the lowest place to cross the Monadnock highlands between the Merrimack and Connecticut Rivers, but that doesn't mean it was flat or easy to bring trains here. The undulating landscape over the next mile and a half demonstrates this well. After a fifty-eight-year history, it was the impact of water—the Great Flood of 1936—that was too much to overcome, as several large trestles were knocked out and never rebuilt. With neglect and time, the wild things began to return to the impounded wetlands, sand pits, and the regenerating forests.

The trail enters wet woodlands and opens to a wide, hard-packed path. Well-spaced stone walls confine it, and the trail rises above a dense forest of hardwoods, hemlocks, and white pines.

Keep an eye out for a sandy "borrow pit" on the right, probably dug out for fill used in the trail's construction. It's dominated by fuzzy, gray-green clumps of reindeer lichen, and pink lady's slippers bloom here in June. It may also serve as a turtle nesting site.

Ahead, the trail dips below the grade and requires a drainage ditch, which the Harris Center maintains regularly, to keep it from flooding. The trail may be rougher here due to drainage issues, and it can be seasonally wet, so those with wheelchairs, strollers, and bikes should take caution.

A Destination Halfway Out

A central feature of the Eastview Rail Trail is an expansive beaver pond.

Around the halfway point, a bend in the trail brings you to the central feature: a sprawling beaver pond. Built along a stone wall and ringed with standing dead trees, it sits tucked behind buckthorn shrubs that grow out of the beaver dam. The view opens just ahead, where a few small benches perch nicely atop the grade. Cobb Hill rises up across the pond in the distance. From here, the pond is prominently in view, as is a small marsh on the left, packed densely with grasses and sedges in the growing season. Consider looking in one direction and taking in the view fully—plants, birds, colors, textures—before turning to absorb the opposite view. It's a subtle way to deepen your observation and slow down.

A longer bench faces the beaver pond, where you can view yellow-blooming spatterdock (water lilies) and the open water, which is home to ducks, beavers, otters, and turtles. In spring and summer, listen for the rolling trill of a great crested flycatcher or the high-pitched shriek of an eastern kingbird. The frog chorus includes bullfrogs, their bass notes rolling repeatedly on hot summer days, as well as spring peepers, green frogs, and pickerel frogs. Dragonflies abound here, too. Watch for a flash of iridescent wings—an ebony jewelwing damselfly floating lazily like a slow-flying fairy. In winter, search for tracks of minks, foxes, coyotes, and deer, as well as otter slides in the snow.

Ebony jewelwing damselflies may be the closest things to fairies that many of us will ever see.
Photo by Frank Gorga (frg-photo.com)

As you continue, look for a brushy area along the trail on the left where wild grapes grow. In June and July, smell the flowers—a scent unlike any other smell in nature, almost as delicious as the grapes themselves in early September. Let your nose lead!

Farther on, the trail dives again through the forest as steep embankments rise on either side. Watch out for soft shoulders and shallow ditches, especially when the trail stays low in the landscape. A hemlock stretch ahead features birds of the deeper woodlands, the most noticeable being hermit thrushes, which may serenade you with their ethereal, flutelike songs.

Search for signs of the granite sheep tunnel that allowed animals to move between pastures under the railroad line. It's largely hidden underground now; oaks drop acorns onto its former pathway. Approaching the western end of the trail, a subtle turnoff for the North Pond Trail junction appears on the right. The soundscape of rushing water may get your attention in times of high water flow. Look for the outlet of North Pond in the form of Nubanusit Brook on the left side of the trail. It shimmers under the sunlight as if it were alive. Many Indigenous peoples understand water as possessing a living spirit, and you might sense its presence when walking this trail.

A granite-lined tunnel once allowed sheep and other livestock to travel between pastures that were bisected by the railroad.

Photo by Brett Amy Thelen

Descend, and maybe enjoy a water view or quick splash on the left. A well-built wooden bridge, last rebuilt in 2022 by the Harrisville Trails Committee, spans the old abutments and provides another fine observation point.

Local or Express

The walk itself is quick—under an hour, even with pauses. But it's worth building a whole morning or afternoon around it. For a longer outing, combine it with an extension to the Jaquith Rail Trail on the Hancock side, or bike the several-mile stretch from the Harris Center to Harrisville. Old Dublin Road, which connects it to Hancock, is among the most scenic roads in the region. A "social road," it was built to help farmers and mill workers get from their houses to the downtown market, church, and meeting house, and it remains a favorite for birders, dog walkers, bikers, horseback riders, and "Sunday drivers."

A National Historic Landmark, Harrisville is still home to a functioning mill. Water from the region's vast water resources and several dammed ponds is used to generate electricity for the mill buildings. The village is nothing short of charming, and it's not just eye candy. There's a great little general store with some of the best home-cooked food in the region, a thriving creative community, local farms, and a small brick library built out over the edge of Harrisville Pond. In summer, end with a dip, and be sure to sample the delicious salads, sandwiches, or sweets at the Harrisville General Store.

The Eastview Rail Trail still connects people and places, just at a slower pace than rail. Walking rail trails is an act of keeping them open and available to all. Nature will reclaim these historic pathways if we allow it to, and there are plenty of stretches where that is the norm. This wonderful trail is an exception.

Harrisville lures visitors in with its history, but it wins them over with an abundance of scenic lakes and ponds, as well as the culinary delights on offer at the Harrisville General Store.

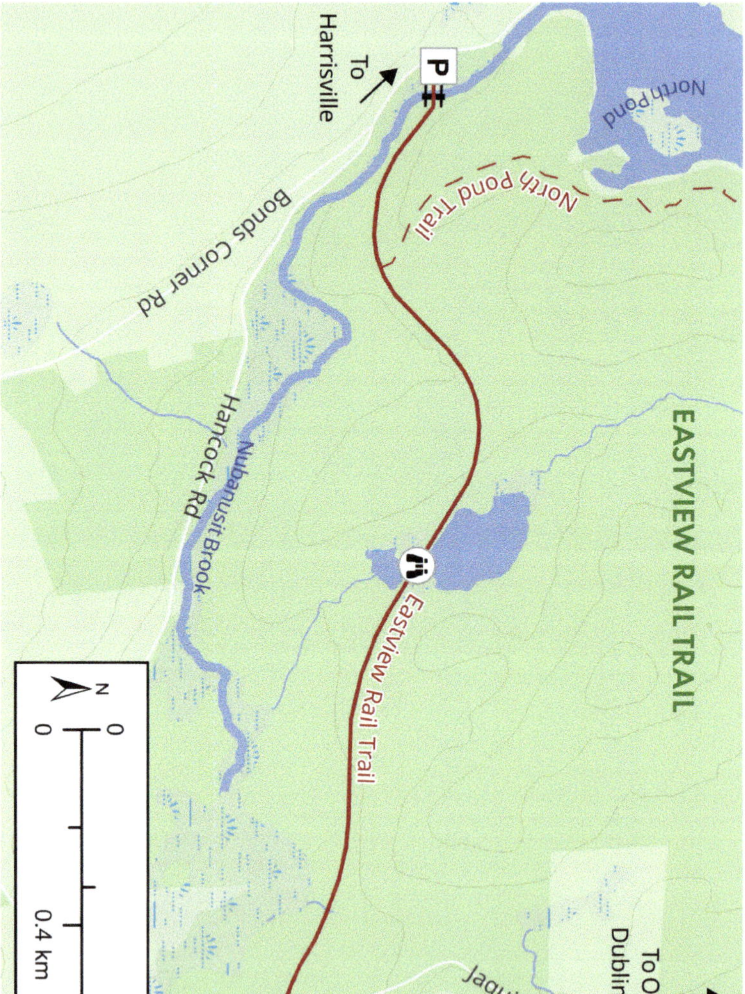
EASTVIEW RAIL TRAIL
North Pond
North Pond Trail
Eastview Rail Trail
Bonds Corner Rd
Hancock Rd
Nubanusit Brook
Jaquith Rd
To Harrisville
To Old Dublin Rd
P
P
N
0
0.4 mi
0
0.4 km

Lay of the Land

TRAILS: 1.4-mile point-to-point trail; flat gravel with little to no elevation change

ACCESS: Parking area off Hancock Road (plowed in winter) and Jaquith Road (small and unplowed)

PERMITTED USES: No motorized vehicles (including e-bikes); dogs OK on short leash at all times

A GREAT PLACE TO: Bike a rail trail and scenic roads to a historic village

INSIDER TIP: You don't need to go high to see fall foliage

DON'T MISS: The cider doughnuts and key lime pie at the Harrisville General Store

CREATURE FEATURE: Snapping turtle

TREASURE HUNT: The sheep tunnel

FAVORITE MONTH: August

SNAPSHOT: The beaver swamp

OWNERSHIP: Harris Center for Conservation Education

DIRECTIONS:

West Parking (Bonds Corner)

East Parking (Jaquith)

OTHER NEARBY MICROS:

- The North Pond Trail starts near the western end of the Eastview Rail Trail and extends 1.6 miles along North Pond and a brook to its junction with the Cobb Hill Trail.
- The Cobb Hill Trail ascends to 1,909 feet, the highest point in Harrisville, and can be combined with the North Pond Trail and the Eastview Trail for a longer hiking loop. It's 1.9 miles to Cobb Hill from the parking area near Merrill's Four Corners in Hancock and 2.5 miles from the parking area on Hancock Road.
- The Jaquith Rail Trail in Harrisville and Hancock connects another mile and a half of rail-turned-trail between Jaquith Road in Hancock and the eastern trailhead of the Eastview Rail Trail. It parallels a large wetland, contains hemlock woodlands, and utilizes a repurposed steel truss bridge under which cardinal flowers bloom in August.

MicroExploring Practices

Wheels and Wanderings

MicroExploring the Monadnock region by bike is one of the most beautiful and rewarding ways to experience local nature. With few cars, endless lakes, and quiet backroads, it's full of wild sights and scenic wonders, and there are biking options for everyone. Its rolling hills push but don't break you, and an array of flat, gravel paths and paved roads cater to the casual peddler. This maze of bucolic back roads through forests, across meadows, around lakes, and through picture-perfect town centers give every ride a feeling of time traveling through a forgotten America.

A bike is a ship that can whisk you on powerful expeditions of discovery. It's not a race, so don't forget to get off the pedals often to explore and allow your senses to take in the views.

The Road on Two Wheels

A road feels entirely different when traveled by bike than when walked. On a bike, the world opens up. The wind touches your face. The road rolls beneath you with momentum. You feel the dips and curves in your body. Distances shrink, and suddenly places you've only driven past become accessible—alive. You can stop when you want, glide when you don't. The landscape speaks differently at speed, and even familiar roads reveal new moods when you meet them on two wheels.

Riding for Joy, Not Speed

Biking offers us a fantastic way to MicroExplore when insects make hiking difficult in late spring and early summer. Some people bike for speed, performance, or exercise—but that's not our style. We prefer a slower, more playful way of riding where the goal isn't distance or sweat, but discovery and fun. We ride to see more, to wander without effort. We stop often—for a photo, a swim, a snack under a tree, or a quiet stroll through an old cemetery. Remember that the more joy you allow in, the more likely you are to get out and ride again. That's how a habit becomes a ritual—and a bike ride becomes a small adventure.

Biking on trails allows you to experience them radically differently from the way you do on foot. It's also a great way to beat the bugs!

With each step the earth heals us, and with each step we heal the earth.

—Thich Nhat Hanh

DOWNTOWN PETERBOROUGH
HOLDING ONTO NATURE

6

Downtown Riverwalk

Peterborough

Walk Summary

The simple motto "A good town to live in" welcomes visitors as they arrive in Peterborough from busy Routes 101 and 202, and it may be a gross understatement. Its historic downtown is compact and contains a low-key arts and culture scene, featuring historical and cultural museums, a brewery, pub, diner, independent bookstore, riverwalk, scenic waterfalls, and the first tax-supported public library in the United States. Nature thrives here, too.

Highlights

- Sample some of the many tastes of downtown Peterborough
- Bask by the confluence of rivers, expressing reverence for the N'dakinna, or homeland, of the Abenaki peoples who have inhabited these lands for millennia
- Witness how water, industry, culture, and nature have shaped this town
- Do a "big sit" or "bioblitz" to see what species you can identify in a small space
- Admire the aerial acrobats: chimney swifts and common nighthawks foraging in the evening sky
- Integrate art, music, and nature in your rhythms, inspired by this confluence of nature and human culture

Park at the Riverwalk parking lot at the confluence of Nubanusit Brook and the Contoocook River. It's easy to observe the natural wonders at this accessible location, which features a pedestrian bridge, paved paths, benches, and picnic tables. Spring features abundant blooms and bountiful birdsong; summer is verdant and full of life in the air and on the water; autumn showcases classic colorful foliage; and winter offers a quaint reprieve from the hustle and bustle to admire the peaceful merging of two waterways. The confluence of these two was vitally important to the Abenaki peoples who traveled along both rivers for trade and communication; archaeological evidence of their presence has been uncovered right here.

This attractive little park is a starting point for a longer walk through town or a destination all in itself. It's well lit for evening strolls or even a night walk; it has benches and a picnic table, too. A newly improved section of lawn beside the bike path is now adorned with attractive tree and shrub plantings. A covered bus stop allows for frequent visits from the local assisted living centers, and the Harris Center offers regular field trips here through its Birding for All program, enabling participants to observe spring migrant warblers, swallows, swifts, fall nighthawks, and more. The Brenner Bridge, formerly the site of a rail bridge, is a lovely place to pause and watch, and it connects this community in more ways than one.

Cross the bridge to enter Depot Square and continue along Nubanusit Brook and around the shops. A well-used amphitheater, home to live music on summer evenings, and an eroded approach to the river are favorite sitting areas. A view south up the Contoocook is framed by a gap in the trees. The river is unusual in that it flows south to north. Notice, depending upon the season, if the trees are leafed out, in bloom, or holding fruit. May's white cherry blossoms give way by late summer to dark red black-cherry fruits, which feed an abundance of wildlife. Black locusts bloom in June and are important trees for pollinators. Breathe in the delicious sweet smell of their dangling white flowers. Continue along the gravel path with river views, shade trees, and a series of benches that invite you to rest, maybe stop to read a bit, and be restored.

Depot Square in fall

Across the parking lot, behind a row of lilacs, you'll see a mural that depicts Peterborough. What stories does it tell? The river trail ends at a small pavilion surrounded by colorful blooms from spring through fall, maintained by volunteers.

Cross the lot to continue the tour, perhaps with a stop at the Toadstool Bookshop, a beloved local establishment, and Aesop's Tables, a favorite hangout and a great place to grab breakfast, lunch, or a sweet snack. Outdoor seating here allows you to enjoy the vibe of the town on a pleasant day. Turn right to follow Depot Street toward the Unitarian church, the Mariposa Museum, and the Peterborough Town Library, all treasured community resources.

A left on School Street brings you past the shops of Depot Square, and, at the corner of School and Grove Streets, you'll see Harlow's Pub on the left, which often hosts live music and always has a lot of heart. Crossing Grove toward the historic downtown area, turn left and head to a bridge where you can view an impressive spillway and dam. Back-to-back catastrophes hit here long ago: the Great Flood of 1936 and the Hurricane of 1938 each took a huge toll on downtown Peterborough and surrounding communities as water overtopped these granite banks.

Grab a beverage outside at Harlow's Pub or Post & Beam Brewery, where you may be rewarded with the sounds of chattering chimney swifts in summer, the smell of fragrant blooms in spring, or the sight of bright fall foliage.

The mighty Nubanusit Brook has spilled over its granite banks, but its power also provides serenity.

Putnam Park

A few steps farther on, step into Putnam Park, the oldest park in Peterborough, created thanks to the vision of Catherine Putnam, who donated the land (then called Putnam Grove) to the town in 1862. Her wish was that it remain a public space, uncluttered by buildings. It was an early example of land conservation for the public good.

The park, dedicated in 1915, is small but large enough for this idyllic town's events. Bounded on one side by Nubanusit Brook, Putnam Park invites you to its different corners, perfect for MicroExploring. A fun challenge here could be to keep what birders call a "patch list," a list of bird species identified within the park's boundaries. This exercise compels you to be still and observant. A "bioblitz," which encourages more mobility, involves identifying not only birds but blooming plants, tiny insects, and more.

Putnam Park is a beloved public space, but it's also easy to carve out your own place.

Paved pathways invite easy walking and are mainly flat. There's a rain garden and an abundance of colorful wildflowers maintained by local volunteers. Stroll with a warm beverage, or take a picnic to this charming little green. Follow the gentle meander of the paths through the kaleidoscope of blooms and past stately oaks and beeches, as well as a linden tree with nine prominent trunks where children play hide-and-seek. Stone benches, placed in both shade and sun, and ample mowed lawn allow you to spread out here and avoid the insect pests of more rural parts of the SuperSanctuary. A tall cut-granite wall is high enough to keep small children from the water's edge but still a good height for others to sit upon to enjoy the rushing current below.

A woods path continues steeply uphill to another impressive spillway, but it traverses private property and is less protected. Skirt the forest edge on the far loop of the trail, getting as close to the woods as one does on this urban walk. Returning to Grove Street, you might wish to stop off at the Post & Beam Brewery for a pint before returning to the lot to complete the loop. A massive yellow birch rains down golden catkins during spring in the establishment's outdoor courtyard, which is perched across from Putnam Park.

Extend your MicroExploring journeys with a night walk!

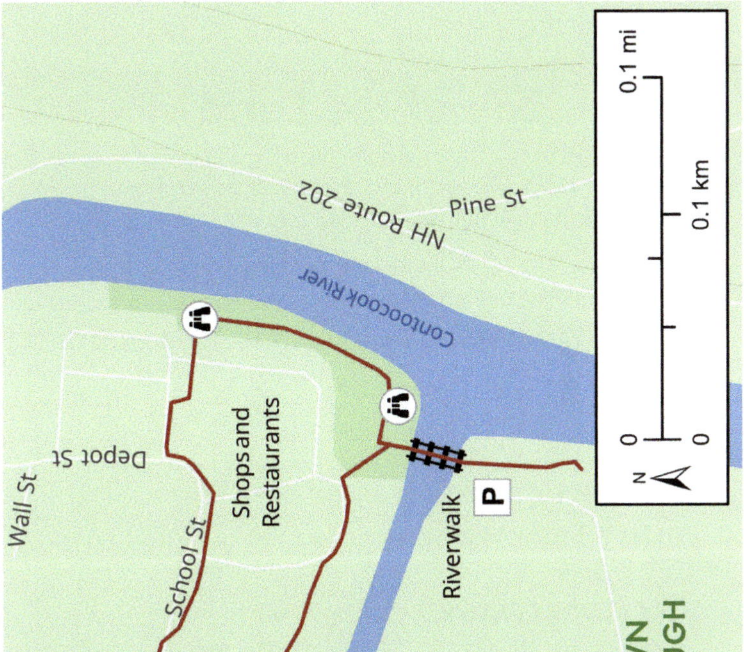

NH Route 202
Pine St
Contoocook River
Wall St
Depot St
School St
Shops and Restaurants
Riverwalk
P
Grove St
Putnam Park
Nubanusit Brook
Vale St
Scott St
Central St
DOWNTOWN PETERBOROUGH
N
0
0.1 mi
0
0.1 km

Lay of the Land

TRAILS: Half-mile loop; mostly paved sidewalks, parking lots, or hard-packed gravel

ACCESS: Parking at Riverwalk parking lot off Grove Street

PERMITTED USES: No motorized vehicles; dogs OK on leash at all times

A GREAT PLACE TO: Write poetry or read a book alongside the water

INSIDER TIP: Enjoy a sit without all the bugs in spring

DON'T MISS: Having a pint outdoors at Harlow's or Post & Beam

CREATURE FEATURE: Chimney swift

TREASURE HUNT: The nine-trunked linden tree in Putnam Park

FAVORITE MONTH: July

SNAPSHOT: The falls from Bridge Street

OWNERSHIP: Town of Peterborough

DIRECTIONS:

MicroExploring Practices

Holding on to Nature

Encounters in nature often leave us feeling lighter, more grounded, and in a better mood. Yet the mind, with its relentless pull toward problems, logic, predicting, and remembering, can drain the very energy we replenish. It's essential to consciously anchor our freshly made positive memories in nature and make them stick.

Noticing What Changes

Tune in to the whispers of your body and the nuances of your emotions as you immerse yourself in nature. Identify the changes in your mood and state of mind as you go through your MicroExplorations. Is your breath slower? Are your cheeks softening into a smile? Is your posture looser and less defensive? These are the signs that something real has shifted. Hang on to them.

On your walk, be conscious of where your eyes are looking. Looking down on the ground leads to internal thinking; looking up forces you to remain present.

Pick one visual from your walk or paddle—a still lake, a twisting tree root, a fallen feather—and link it to the feeling you cultivated in your walk. Let it become a symbolic memory, and draw on that memory to bring about that feeling later.

Anchors and Reminders

Photography is the magic of freezing time. Images from your walks become anchors, keeping the memory of those experiences alive. Give yourself license to take as many photos of your journey as you like—and not just for sharing. Scrolling back through them can reawaken the mental and spiritual state you felt on the trail, like squeezing more juice from the moment. If you went on the walk with someone, make it a practice to share your favorite photos a day or two later—not as a recap but as a way to step back into the mood together.

Bring home a token. Beautiful small natural objects you pick up on a walk, like a rock, pine cone, feather, or leaf, can serve as a reminder that you were there. Place it on a windowsill, car dash, or your desk. Let it sit as a powerful symbol that the moment mattered. And on your next walk, bring it back to the forest to return it to nature in gratitude.

The mind loves to circle. Feed the fire with mental replays of the beauty of your walks and time in nature. Make the loop work for you, and keep feeling the peace you found outside.

Accept the gift nature is offering you. Instead of just walking through it, mindfully interact with the beauty around you through touch and play. Nature has the power to turn into anything you imagine: from a giant friend you can hug to a canvas with free supplies you can create art with.

The press of my foot to the earth springs a hundred affections.

—Walt Whitman

PITCHER MOUNTAIN 7
THE BEAUTY OF REPETITION

Sudden Summit

Stoddard

Walk Summary

There's a small summit in Stoddard, conserved for all to enjoy, where views are endless, blueberries abound, and shrubland birds sing. Its preservation and fire history are unique in how they've shaped the land for wildlife and people to use. Visit often to experience awe and get a taste of why this is one of the sweetest places around.

Highlights

- Smell the sweet fragrance of blooming shrubs in late spring
- Search for your special place in a magical Norway spruce grove
- Pick wild blueberries with a date, and watch the sunset over Vermont
- Listen for bobolinks singing in the field, eastern towhees *"drinking-their-tea,"* and white-throated sparrows singing *"O-sweet-Canada"*
- In warm months, feel the cooler air and a gentle breeze blowing across the summit
- Bask on the granite outcrop and watch hawks overhead

At 2,162 feet in elevation, Pitcher Mountain is a small mountain by New Hampshire standards. But from its open top and historic fire tower, you'll get a 360-degree view that rivals that of much taller summits. The hike to the summit is under half a mile and gains only a few hundred feet. Nowhere else in the region can you see so far while sweating so little!

An early spring view from the fire tower.

The drive to Pitcher Mountain from the east or south offers a scenic prelude to the hike itself, taking you through the small village of Stoddard and past Island Pond. Ascend on Route 123 through the village, climbing through dense hardwood forests until you reach Pitcher Mountain Farm. Look for shaggy Scottish Highland cattle and bison in the pastures, as well as wildlife such as turkeys, kestrels, deer, or even a bear. The trailhead for Pitcher Mountain is on the right and overflow parking is possible along the shoulder, but this road moves fast, so use caution.

The Ascent

From the trailhead, the wide gravel road to the right is part of the Monadnock-Sunapee Greenway (MSG) Trail and perfect for walking side by side. A faster, more direct way uphill is straight ahead, but this trail is often eroded and is generally less diverse. A gated road to the left leads to Hubbard Hill, and another section of the MSG Trail, but this is nice to save for the return trip.

As you start out, you'll traverse a young mixed forest of northern hardwoods, spruce, and pine with a variety of understory shrubs, including mountain and striped maples. Save

Colorful American kestrels hunt the open fields of Pitcher Mountain Farm during warmer months.

Photo by Susan Kline

your meadow viewing for the second vantage point following a short, steep stretch. From the flat rocks (and beyond the electric fencing) you can see Monadnock rising to the south and the Wapack Range's prominent peaks just above its ridgeline to the southeast. In the middle distance, the hilly SuperSanctuary unfolds before your eyes. In spring, the color patchwork of emerging leaves rivals autumn's finery. Scan the fields for bobolinks, savannah sparrows, or a hovering kestrel. If the sun is what you've come to find, there will be more up ahead, but this brief interlude with partial shade is a welcome place to ponder how this landscape came to be so green and conserved.

Though the summit of Pitcher Mountain is owned by the State of New Hampshire as a fire-watching station, the land surrounding it is part of the privately owned Andorra Forest. Jim and Mary Faulkner began purchasing forest land in 1937 and over time assembled what became one of the largest private landholdings in the state. The family donated a conservation easement on the entire 11,500 acres to the Forest Society of New Hampshire in 1990, and today, it is managed for wildlife, low-impact timber production, and wilderness. Andorra is one of the gateways of the SuperSanctuary, connecting fifteen thousand additional conserved acres to the north and west.

Pushing on, the final ascent passes through gnarly apple trees and low spruces—signs of past agriculture and fire. This short, steeper section has a few bigger steps, and a hiking stick will help in wet or muddy conditions. Due to exposure and elevation, snow and mud often persist into late April. There is a sweet spot between mud season and black flies, but a visit in May or June may be accelerated in pace by hordes of biting insects.

Taste the Summit

Dominated by rocky ledges and shrubs, the summit itself is worth savoring. To locals, Pitcher is known for its abundant meadows of pick-your-own blueberries. Its summer soundscape includes the plunk of blueberries plopping into buckets. Some fifty acres of blueberries are now managed here through fire and mechanical means. The Andorra Forest leaves a collection box next to the parking lot for an honor-system payment.

From the base of the fire tower—one of sixteen remaining lookout points in New Hampshire—take in the full panorama of Vermont's snowy ski slopes to the west, Mount Ascutney rising alone to the north, and countless hills and valleys rolling out below. A view from the fire tower's platform is a must if you're comfortable with heights.

The sight of the sea of blueberry bushes flowering in spring is nearly as enjoyable as the berries' taste in summer.

The fire tower serves a reminder of the Great Marlow-Stoddard Fire, which began on April 28, 1941, when a "perfect storm" of dry, hot spring conditions with ample fuel—downed trees from the 1938 hurricane—ignited the largest fire in New Hampshire's recorded history. Winds ushered it south and over the summit of Pitcher Mountain, burning the fire tower. Thousands of volunteers jumped into action and helped save Pitcher Mountain Farm. Thankfully, a late snow and rain fell, and winds died down on April 30, extinguishing the blaze, but not before it burned twenty-seven thousand acres, including almost half of Marlow's and Stoddard's land area.

Today, due to its open summit and location, Pitcher is one of the best places in New Hampshire to view hawks and other raptors in the spring. From mid-March to early May, you may glimpse eye-level migration of bald eagles, broad-winged and red-shouldered hawks, or a rare golden eagle. Stand south of the fire tower (which serves nicely as a wind block) and face Monadnock, scanning the horizon for birds rising into the air. Eastern towhees, dark-eyed juncos, white-throated sparrows, and a variety of warbler species sing from the shrubby summit between May and July.

Looping Down

When you're done exploring the summit, bypass the steep and rocky trail that returns to the parking lot and instead take the scenic and diverse route down via the MSG Trail. Highbush blueberries dominate in this rocky, acidic soil, providing good picking in July and August. Footpaths through the berry-producing shrubs are maintained by human feet and those of black bears, the large, berry-filled scat of which is a familiar sight in summer and fall. The shrublands in bloom are fragrant, ablaze with white flowers and abuzz with pollinators. The blooming shrubs include chokeberry, highbush blueberry, cherries, and mountain holly. And look for rhodora, or bog azalea, which glows magenta in mid to late May before leafing out. This stunning native shrub is a sight to behold in boggy wetlands as well as on high-elevation summits, and it is a rare treat to see so many together.

Two northern shrub species thrive near Pitcher's summit: rhodora (left) shows off stunning blooms in May, and mountain holly (right) bursts forth with vibrant berries in July.

Soon the trail drops into a serene red spruce forest on the mountain's northern slope. The contrast is striking—suddenly quiet, shaded, and still. The air is cooler and smells of the north.

Red squirrels scold from the trees, and nipped-off spruce cones and clipped twigs litter the trail. At a T junction, a right turn onto a gravel road takes you 1.5 miles to Hubbard Hill and its many acres of cultivated blueberries, while a left returns you safely to the parking lot. Tall Norway spruces, planted a century ago, are featured on the right. Poke into their tidy rows if you're curious to explore this magical-feeling forest.

Though this hike lacks water features, Cold Spring Pond is just under a mile away. There you can launch a canoe, fish, or scan for one of the region's most reliably spotted nesting pairs of common loons.

A four-season destination, Pitcher Mountain becomes a rugged hike or ski during winter.

Photo by Julie Brown

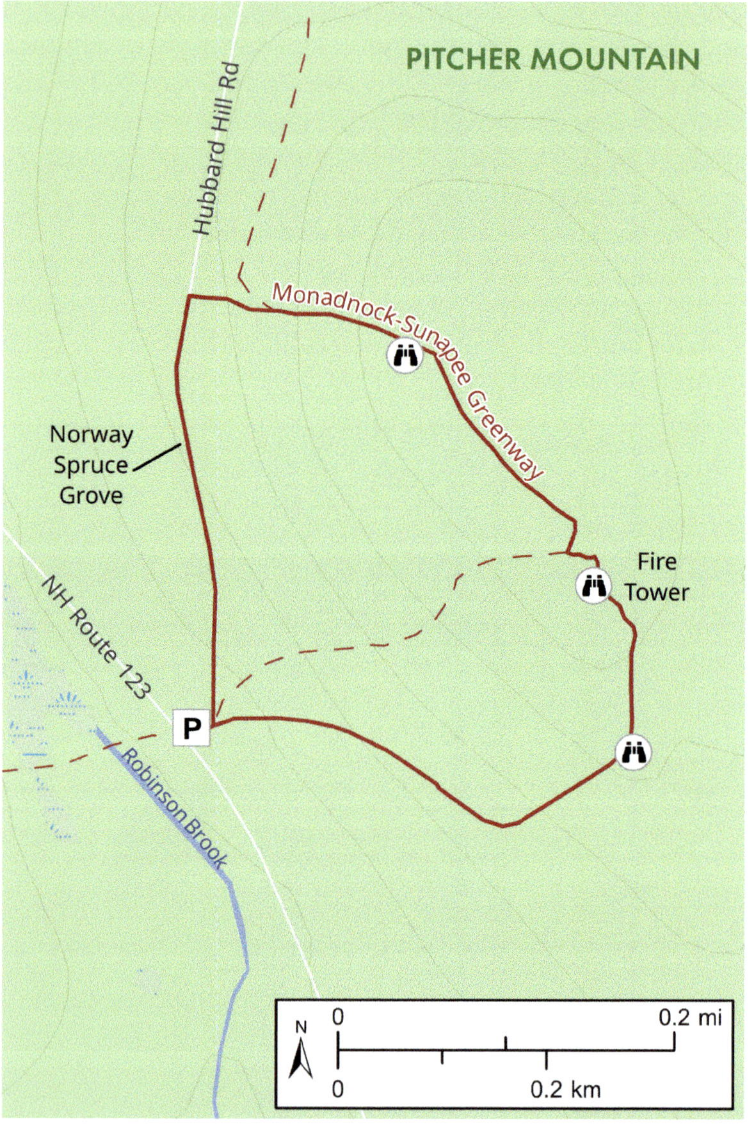
PITCHER MOUNTAIN
Hubbard Hill Rd
Monadnock-Sunapee Greenway
Norway Spruce Grove
Fire Tower
NH Route 123
P
Robinson Brook
N
0
0.2 mi
0
0.2 km

Lay of the Land

TRAILS: One-mile loop with miles of additional trails; moderately steep ascent; rocky ground at the summit

ACCESS: Parking area off Route 123 between Stoddard and Marlow

PERMITTED USES: No motorized vehicles; dogs OK on short leash at all times

A GREAT PLACE TO: Enjoy tasty wild blueberries on a scenic summit

INSIDER TIP: Bring a date to enjoy the sunset over Vermont

DON'T MISS: Seeing the blueberries and other wild shrubs in bloom in May

CREATURE FEATURE: Eastern towhee

TREASURE HUNT: Find fairies in the magic Norway spruce forest

FAVORITE MONTH: April

SNAPSHOT: View across pastures to the SuperSanctuary's hills

OWNERSHIP: Andorra Forest and the State of New Hampshire

DIRECTIONS:

MicroExploring Practices

The Beauty of Repetition

The only true voyage . . . is not to go to new landscapes, but to see with different eyes.

—Marcel Proust

Walking a path that you've traversed many times before is like rewatching an old favorite movie, in which each time you discover more and more details you hadn't noticed before. In a world infected with the incessant need for the new, repeating adventures might seem boring to some, or perhaps spark a fear of missing out on unknown new experiences. But to the MicroExplorer, revisiting familiar trails and natural sites is one of the most enriching and exciting things you can do.

The Gift of the Familiar

Our nervous system appreciates familiar trails because it can let go of the subconscious fear of getting lost or finding unwelcome surprises. Knowing you are somewhere familiar will relax your body and allow you to take in even more of the healing properties of nature and the medicine of the present moment. Don't play the adventure down because you've already done it! Instead of focusing your energy on where you are going, notice what has changed. Nature is an ever-changing kaleidoscope: a flower that blooms one day a year, frogs that come out only when it rains, birds that migrate past on a specific week of the year. Once you train your eyes to look for the new in the old, you'll begin finding excitement all around you.

Experimenting with Perspective

Try walking the trail in reverse, visiting it at different times of the day, in different seasons and during different weather systems. Bring different people to accompany you. Walking the trail with a friend, your children, or your dog will shift the experience and offer fresh ways of seeing the same path.

If you've always hiked it, try biking, boating, or even barefooting it. If you always walk with binoculars, try bringing a hand lens and zoom in on flowers and insects instead, or bring only your eyes and senses.

When the relentless turmoil and pressures of the world weigh heavily on your mind and soul, consider offering yourself the gentle balm of familiar paths. Embrace the repeatable rhythm, the inherent comfort, and the reassuring safety found within your usual walks and trails. This consistent connection with a known natural space can act as a soothing prescription, providing a sanctuary where the anxieties of the outside world soften and a sense of inner peace can gently take root.

By returning to the familiar, you'll actually make more discoveries and go deeper. You're never simply hiking the same trail again.

WELCH FAMILY FARM AND FOREST

8

THE GIFT OF TIME

Historic Farm Walk

Hancock

In all of nature, there can be nothing more expressive than silence.

—John Hay

Walk Summary

Tucked away on a wooded hillside just off Hancock's main road, the Welch Farm is a destination on the way to other places. As a result, few seem to visit this little roadside gem. Though nature has reclaimed it, a historic farming history still hangs on if you know where—and how—to look for it. Stop in to witness both, side by side.

Highlights

- Reap the rewards of a "twenty-minute fix" by basking in the evening glow with a view of hills and fields
- Reflect on the legacy of Jack Ware, a formerly enslaved man, and the Due family, early free Black residents, as they endured hardships farming this land two hundred years ago
- Come in search of serenity, introspection, and connection to the past and present
- Look for great blue herons hiding among old stumps in the beaver pond
- Listen for frogs singing from vernal pools, a gusty wind howling through the trees, hoarse ravens croaking in flight overhead, or the resonant drumming of a pileated woodpecker
- Smell the earthy scent around the beaver pond: castor mounds and the distinctive odor of beavers

We manage to visit here once or twice each spring, and again in fall, perhaps because we know it will be lost during winter, as the parking lot isn't plowed. It's special to be the first—and last—visitors a place might see for a while. It might make the wildlife easier to come upon, and if you walk here regularly, you'll surely be the first to lay down tracks most mornings.

A Path to Black History

Within a few hundred feet of the trailhead and beyond the gate, the grassy roadway spills into a large brushy field on either side, which is mowed periodically. It is full of raspberry and blackberry brambles, vines, and shrubby regeneration that is managed in rotation with other young forest patches to create a mosaic of young forest conditions. The occasional remnant apple tree and the small-needled junipers that grow in abandoned clearings are living reminders of the land's agricultural past. A beloved snag—a huge, lone dead pine that once towered over the cut field at a noticeable lean—now adorns the brushy pasture and enters its final act above ground as habitat for wildlife and a source of nourishing nutrients to the soil.

Just along the path are two smaller hardwood trees, which contrast with other nearby trees in their unusual branching structure. Low-growing, full-bodied, and with upward-facing branches, these twins are southern catalpas, perhaps planted near the old homestead in remembrance or for shade. Maybe both. Everything had purpose back then. Visit the catalpas from late June into July to enjoy their large, showy white flowers.

Behind them is a plaque—Hancock's first and (so far) only marker along the Black Heritage Trail of New Hampshire—that pays homage to a mixed-race family who farmed this land over two hundred years ago. James and Hannah Due, along with a man named Jack Ware, endured the hard labor of New England farming and harassment by the local church. Jack was captured as a child in Africa and enslaved on this continent, as were so many other African people. After gaining his freedom, he settled on land given by the Due family. He died at around one hundred

Twin catalpa trees mark the entrance to a grassy path leading to the Black Heritage Trail marker that honors the Due family.

years old in 1826. Nearby Jack's Pond in Hancock is named in his honor. Today, those same pastures hum with birdsong and bees, and the woods invite a different kind of visitor: those seeking connection to something deeper.

Back on the road, the path rises gently (it can be muddy in spring), framed by double stone walls. Turn around and you'll see the round summit of Skatutakee Mountain on the left and the triangular peak of Thumb Mountain on the right. This may be as far as we need to go some days. If there's a warm sun and good visibility, we might linger here a bit longer. Take the same view across the seasons, and see how it changes. Photograph it, paint it, or simply observe. Try to discern tree species by their bud colors on a late April morning, or gawk at the stunning foliage on this hillside in October. Or perhaps take in the sun dipping over these western hills on a quick stop during an evening commute.

Relics of a bygone farming era remain here in stone walls, cleared pastures, and the occasional piece of farm equipment such as this rusted hay rake.

In the 1860s, the Welch family (originally from Ireland) began farming here, raising cows, chickens, pigs, and vegetables, and sugaring an eight-hundred-tap maple stand. By the turn of the century, the farm had become a boardinghouse and was instrumental in pioneering farm tourism. Well over a hundred years later, the same family donated this land to the Forest Society, which enables us to enjoy it today as conserved and open to the public.

A rusted chain—one end of which is now swallowed by the bark of an old oak—once blocked the road ahead. Look closely at chest height and you'll see a dark belt around its trunk, a mark from lead arsenate used during a spongy moth outbreak in the 1980s. A scar of chemical warfare to combat biological warfare, quietly absorbed by time, it's not a common mark in the woods.

Old Woods Road to the Beaver Swamp

Veer left at the T junction of an old woods road—once the main connection between Hancock and Stoddard—bounded by well-built stone walls and lined by big oaks, sugar maples, and other hardwoods. Acorns are everywhere in a good mast year (and the following year, after the snow melts). You may notice tracks of deer, coyotes, and humans along a narrow corridor.

As the fields around you fade into forest, the road narrows with vegetation growth; look for a left turn (marked in yellow) across an opening in the stone wall. The trail is narrow in the brushy field, but the payoff is worthwhile. Just before the trail enters the woods is a fine, distant view of Pack Monadnock across the field to the southeast.

The woods start out young here, a result of recent forest management history, which will continue under the Forest Society's careful stewardship. A minor brook crossing, the outflow of a beaver pond, can be easily navigated in most conditions with a little rock-hopping. Ahead lies the source, a prominent feature of this trail network. Dammed by a stone wall and elevated above the trail grade, this pond is well situated for exploring.

Beaver ponds with standing dead trees are excellent places to observe wildlife.

A beaver lodge stands out as a pyramid of sticks on the pond; sometimes there are several active ones. Beavers are cyclical, and they will abandon ponds in search of food resources if their choice shrub and hardwood saplings stop growing. Here, despite conifers dominating the far side of the pond, there's no sign the beavers are on the way out anytime soon. Castor scent mounds on the pond's shoreline and ample browse nearby indicate their continued presence, as do mud and fresh blond sticks atop their winter homes.

Alongside the lodges are numerous dead, standing trees, relics of a time before beavers began transforming this landscape. Once flooded, the trees likely became prime real estate for great blue heron nests. At this point any "rookery" is long gone, as most of the supporting upper branches have fallen. A "ghost forest" this is not, however, as it teems with life on all levels. Decomposers break down the wood; cavity-nesting birds like wood ducks, tree swallows, and great crested flycatchers call. Below, in the swamp, bullfrogs chorus in their resonating baritones in June and July, while the shrill notes of red-shouldered hawks cascade from above. Stand awhile at dusk or dawn, perhaps in the shoulder seasons when mosquitoes won't keep you moving along.

Beyond the Pond

Beyond the pond, the trail continues through older woods—hemlocks, pines, and hardwoods—quiet and shaded, rich with ethereal songs of hermit thrushes and home to vocal barred owls. Be on the lookout for where a powerful microburst tore through in 2017, leaving snapped trunks and tipped giants in its wake. The impressive devastation can be seen along a fifteen-mile swath through two counties—but you'll have to look hard as forest regeneration is well underway.

Up ahead, a massive three-trunked white pine towers over a stone wall, visible from the woods road. Its size and location suggest that it has been left to grow since the sheep-pasture days of the nineteenth century. This trail continues and intersects with the now discontinued Kulish Forest Trail on the right. The trail is still possible to follow although difficult in places; the markers have been removed and it sees little traffic. Continuing ahead brings you to the trail's terminus at the junction of Route 123 and Clark Farm Road.

Stumbling upon a massive white pine off the main trail is a typically joyful side effect of MicroExploring. This particular giant was likely a pasture shade tree for sheep early in the last century.

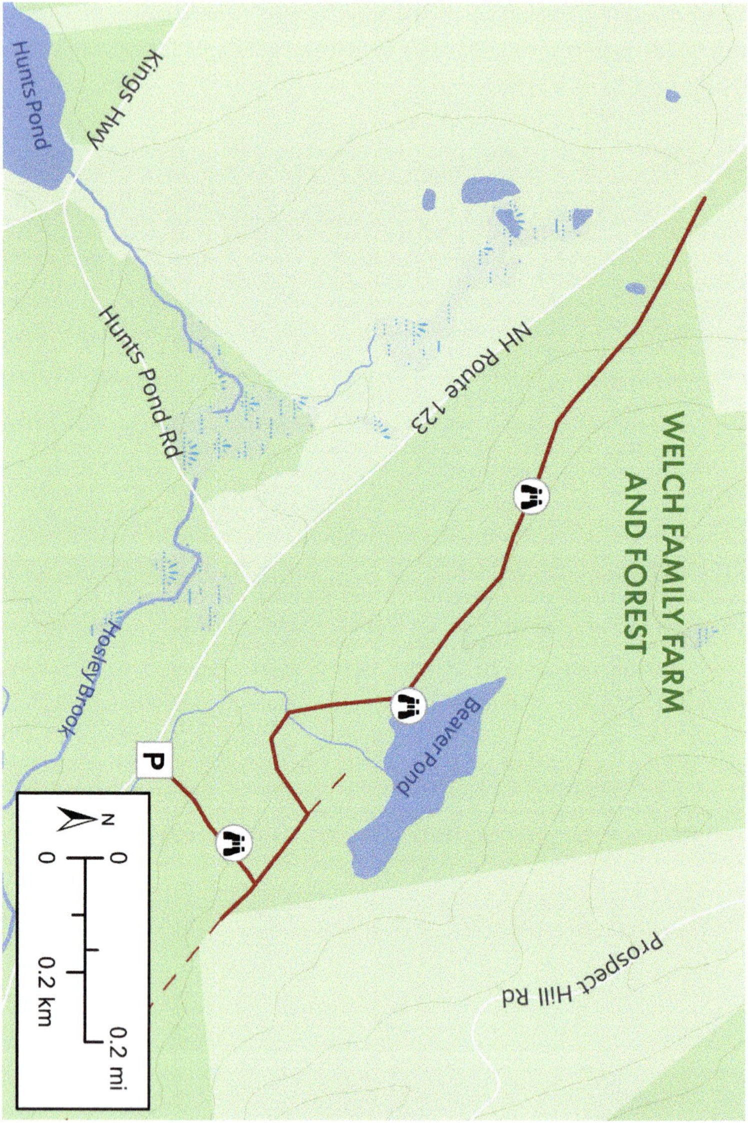
Hunts Pond
Kings Hwy
Hunts Pond Rd
NH Route 123
WELCH FAMILY FARM
AND FOREST
Hosley Brook
Beaver Pond
Prospect Hill Rd
P
N
0
0.2 mi
0
0.2 km

Lay of the Land

TRAILS: One mile of trail; some elevation gain but mostly gentle terrain

ACCESS: Small roadside pull-off along Route 123 north of Hancock center (please don't block the gate; not plowed during winter)

PERMITTED USES: Foot traffic only; dogs OK under control at all times

A GREAT PLACE TO: Observe a mosaic of habitats in close proximity

INSIDER TIP: Explore during the shoulder seasons

DON'T MISS: The Black Heritage Trail marker

CREATURE FEATURE: Great blue heron

TREASURE HUNT: A rusty horse-drawn hay rake along the woods road to the east

FAVORITE MONTH: May

SNAPSHOT: The massive three-trunked white pine along the woods road; take a pic with a person for scale

OWNERSHIP: Society for the Protection of New Hampshire Forests

DIRECTIONS:

MicroExploring Practices

The Gift of Time

One of the core tenets of MicroExploring is that Micros can be brief. Their short length makes them easy to weave into daily life—no need to block off hours or rearrange your schedule. The beauty of this is consistency: when nature time feels doable, you'll do it more often. And the more often you go, the more it becomes a way of life.

Time is a human-made construct that disintegrates upon contact with the wild. Terms like *old, young, today,* and *tomorrow* bear no meaning amid nature's vastness.

Breaking the Busy Myth

The most important commitment you can make as a Micro-Explorer is to challenge thought patterns that whisper suggestions that you are too busy to take time to spend in nature each week. When your mind insists there's no time because you are busy and stressed, that's exactly when you need it the most. Reverse the belief that nature is a luxury, because it is a necessity for our bodies and minds, as important as breathing air or drinking water.

It's ironic that the times we need nature the most—when we're drained, down, or overwhelmed—are often the moments we feel least able to go outside. But if we push past the heaviness, even a short walk can lift our mood and restore our energy, rather than deplete it further. Once you begin to notice that it works, you'll trust it. And once you trust it, you'll begin to make it a part of how you care for yourself—consistently, instinctively, and without hesitation.

Transforming Intention into Habit

Allow yourself to make a conscious effort to reprogram yourself with a new set of personal guidelines dictating your relationship with nature. These statements are private and should speak to you clearly and powerfully. Some examples follow:

- Taking time for nature isn't a break from a successful day but a sign of it.
- Nature time each week is nonnegotiable. It's part of how we operate.

- We always forget how much we need it—until we go. Then we remember, deeply.
- Nature doesn't take time—it gives time back to us.
- Going outside is not an escape—it's a return.
- A few minutes in stillness can undo hours of noise.
- Nature can be a "twenty-minute fix" or a "one-hour wonder."

The peace of the wild has the power to both disarm and anchor us.

Treat nature time like any other important appointment in your week. Add it to your calendar, send an invite to your Micro buddy so you don't forget it, and defend it in your calendar once it's there. Knowing that in the future you have an appointment with nature will motivate you to keep being productive because you know there is a lovely scheduled rest stop coming up.

Don't rely on the weather. Some of the most magical moments in nature happen when the weather isn't ideal—mist rising from a lake, a sudden sunbeam after a passing shower, or a rainbow breaking through the rain clouds. Don't wait for blue skies or permission from your weather app.

Even a few minutes in nature can make a real difference in your well-being. No time for a walk? No problemo. Gift yourself the scenic route on your drive home and take a road you have never taken before. While driving, keep an eye out for new trails and hidden places and add them to your list of Micros to explore. Take a short walk before or after a meal, even if only for ten minutes. Step away from the screens and wander outside in the evening to peek at the stars before bed. Looking up at a star-filled night sky is one of the best ways to gain perspective as we float together through the galaxy on this beautiful planet.

Let the forest untether your spirit from the modern world.

Look deep into nature, and then you will understand everything better.

—Albert Einstein

THE MILL POND AND WILLARD POND

9

MICRO BUDDIES

Shoreline Sanctuary

Antrim and Hancock

Walk Summary

Willard Pond Wildlife Sanctuary is a conservation cornerstone of the SuperSanctuary. Both its namesake pond and the smaller, neighboring Mill Pond are rich resources, naturally and historically, and contain stories as deep as their waters. A visit here is a return to our roots, a time of pureness and simplicity, and a place to experience wildness up close.

Highlights

- Combine leisure with adventure by taking a swim or paddle on Willard Pond
- Listen for loons, and keep an eye out for porcupines under massive boulder piles
- Embody the feeling of sanctuary—a safe place for all to enjoy
- Relive memories or make new ones, alone or with a friend
- Admire fall foliage around the Mill Pond's scenic shoreline
- Smell the spicebush leaves
- Explore a balanced rock and a centuries-old sawmill site

Near the end of a long unpaved road past rustic camps and rural houses, an unassuming granite boulder on the right serves as a gateway to the sanctuary. An engraving here honors Elsa Tudor dePierrefeu, who established the original 650-acre sanctuary in 1967. A pacifist, she recognized the value of sacred places and the importance of protecting wildlife. Decades later, New Hampshire Audubon continues to steward this parcel, which has tripled in size. This early seed of conserved land was an anchor for land protection efforts and was instrumental in the SuperSanctuary's origin story.

Mill Pond Trail

Most people who visit Willard come for the pond itself, but there is so much more to discover on the miles of trails along ridgetops and shorelines. Perhaps most overlooked is a small treasure hidden in plain sight across from the parking lot and behind a row of trees and dense shrubs. This is the tiny Mill Pond, and a short trail circles it.

The loop hike includes a short road walk from the parking lot and kiosk. This trail can be explored in each direction and each season; however, two brook crossings can be challenging during snow and ice. The trail's entrances are subtle and concealed along the main road. The north entrance of the loop is accessed directly across from the more popular Tudor Trail, which runs nearly a mile along the rocky, western edge of Willard Pond. Rocky woodlands and a shrubby shoreline greet you as you step onto the Mill Pond Trail, which moves from hardwoods to pine and eventually to hemlock forests as the loop progresses. The birdlife reflects these habitats, too; as the woods grow darker, summer songs of ovenbirds and red-eyed vireos give way to winter wrens and blue-headed vireos. Moose, bobcats, and bears roam freely here, their sign typically the only evidence of their passing through.

Highbush blueberry and other wetland plants lead to the first brook crossing just a few hundred feet from the larger pond's dam. A concrete spillway controls water flow, and by June or July, diminished flow usually calms the rushing brook. Kids may especially enjoy the challenge of rock-hopping. Verdant royal ferns emerge out of the water in spring, and stunning scarlet cardinal flowers bloom here within arm's reach in late summer. Look for spicebush, an uncommon wetland shrub with a delicious smell, as you cross. Break off a leaf, crush it up, and sniff! A butterfly called the spicebush swallowtail relies on this host plant near the northern end of its range here.

Notice the forest change across the brook. Tall hemlocks tower over a parklike open understory devoid of vegetation. They've been here awhile. Serenity takes hold near this part of the loop furthest from the road. Orient yourself to your wooded surroundings, relying on your sense of hearing (can you still hear the brook flowing?) and sight (can you see how the understory vegetation grows denser closer to the pond's edge?).

Looping back into view of the Mill Pond on your right, you may see a pair of low, smooth boulders, one with a complete split that halves it perfectly. Think about the incredible forces at work over twelve thousand years needed to split this granite. A closer inspection of the rocks in this area reveals rough texture and large embedded crystals of granite, signs of a slow cooling process when this rock was still in liquid form. Take this stretch slowly, pausing at the small "window" views of the pond and surrounding forest. Perhaps an otter or beaver may make an appearance if you're still enough. Abundant evidence of blond, cut stumps and chewed logs suggests beaver activity in recent years.

Continuing ahead, you'll intersect with the beginning of the trail that takes hikers steadily up Goodhue Hill, where New Hampshire Audubon has conducted forest management to promote diverse bird habitats and increase climate resilience.

The two-hundred-year-old Hatch Sawmill must have been impressive in its time. The Mill Pond Trail highlights the remains of its tall dam and lengthy spillway.

Hatch Sawmill

At the next footbridge sit the remains of a historic dam associated with the Hatch Sawmill, built by David Low of Antrim in 1825. The impressive stonework is evident in the high wall and the long, narrow raceway which leads south across the bridge to the mill building itself, an excellent example of an early saw and turning mill. According to local records, at that time the town had two taverns, two stores, seven sawmills, six gristmills, two cloth mills, two carding mills for processing wool, a bark mill to make chemicals for tanning, and three tanneries. The Hatch mill was built for the subsistence needs of just one family, but today it provides a public benefit to those who walk this trail.

At just over two thousand feet in elevation, Bald Mountain rises over the Mill Pond from a clearing. Pause here, take a photo, or sketch this awe-inspiring scene, thinking back to the importance of water and place in the early 1800s—and much earlier, before the dam was built, when Abenaki people fished these waters and hunted on these lands.

Take care when crossing the bridge (which may run over with water at times) and in navigating the old spillway, and use the rope to safely cross along the narrow path. The stone channel and walls funneled water to the sawmill, the remains of which stand just downstream on private land. A final footbridge crosses the impressively long, straight raceway, and the trail rises over a rocky stretch in the hemlocks. Look for the peanut-shaped droppings of porcupines underneath boulders that they've frequented for decades. Before you spot them, though, you might smell the musty scent of a fresh den.

Willard Pond

Completing the loop, you'll pass a barn on the left where New Hampshire Audubon protects and monitors a colony of bats. The parking lot is to the right along with the Tamposi trailhead, which may beckon you up Bald Mountain, a scenic gem of the region. Either way, across the road is an impressive balanced boulder that is worth a quick peek. And, of course, any visit here *must* include a short walk to the 107-acre, heart-shaped pond at the end of the road. Rare is a place that embodies such deep personal connections for residents and visitors alike yet remains unspoiled. Everyone who visits this special pond leaves with a memory—a close encounter with a loon, a first kiss, a special moment in time. The immensity of this landscape will

The balanced rock is a favorite spot for a photo and awe.

dwarf you. Though many have set foot on the same rocks and paddled the same waters, there's room enough to find sanctuary and create your own unique experience.

Busy on hot summer days between July Fourth and Labor Day, Willard is a destination for locals and visitors alike. While you might be hard-pressed to find a quiet spot on the shoreline trails this time of year, it's a spectacular all-season location, and in other months the parking lot is empty. Winter brings solitude on snowshoes or a ski across the frozen and windswept pond (it's often windy here and can be biting on days with a brisk north wind). In late April, a rush of die-hard fly fishermen hit Willard Pond in their float tubes, hip waders, and brown fishing vests to catch recently stocked trout of several species, trying to fish them out before the ospreys, bald eagles, and common loons do. A loon pair nests on the pond each summer and delights visitors with their haunting calls and animated antics. The pond's impressive clarity is like few others in the state, sometimes allowing boaters to view loons underneath them diving for fish. Please give the loons their space, though!

Common loons have nested at Willard Pond for many years, delighting visitors who watch and listen to them as they fish and raise their young.

Photo by Brian Reilly

Check along the shoreline during blueberry season in July and August for a trailside snack, and enjoy the autumn glow of purplish-red blueberry leaves in late fall after most other species have dropped their leaves. In winter, these same bushes are gray, scraggly, and gnarled. Search for huge water snakes by the old stone dam past the picnic table, and admire the blooming laurels and rhododendrons here, the latter of which were planted next to a former cabin owned by Forbes Leland, the

A boulder may be an island, but it isn't alone. At least seven species of trees or plants grow on this particular pyramid-shaped rock. Buttonbush, pink lady's slipper, and bottle gentian (bottom, left to right) are just some of the flowering plants you're likely to encounter along Willard's shorelines in season.

grandson of Elsa Tudor dePierrefeu. Leland helped complete the sanctuary his grandmother started; as the story goes, he was spurred to do so by a vision that came to him in a dream. An engraving on a granite boulder along the shoreline memorializes him—just one of Willard's many secrets that unfold to the attentive MicroExplorer.

This gem of the region is the promise of conservation, which leaves something for our grandchildren's grandchildren to enjoy, cherish, and steward.

Bald Mountain from the Mill Pond.

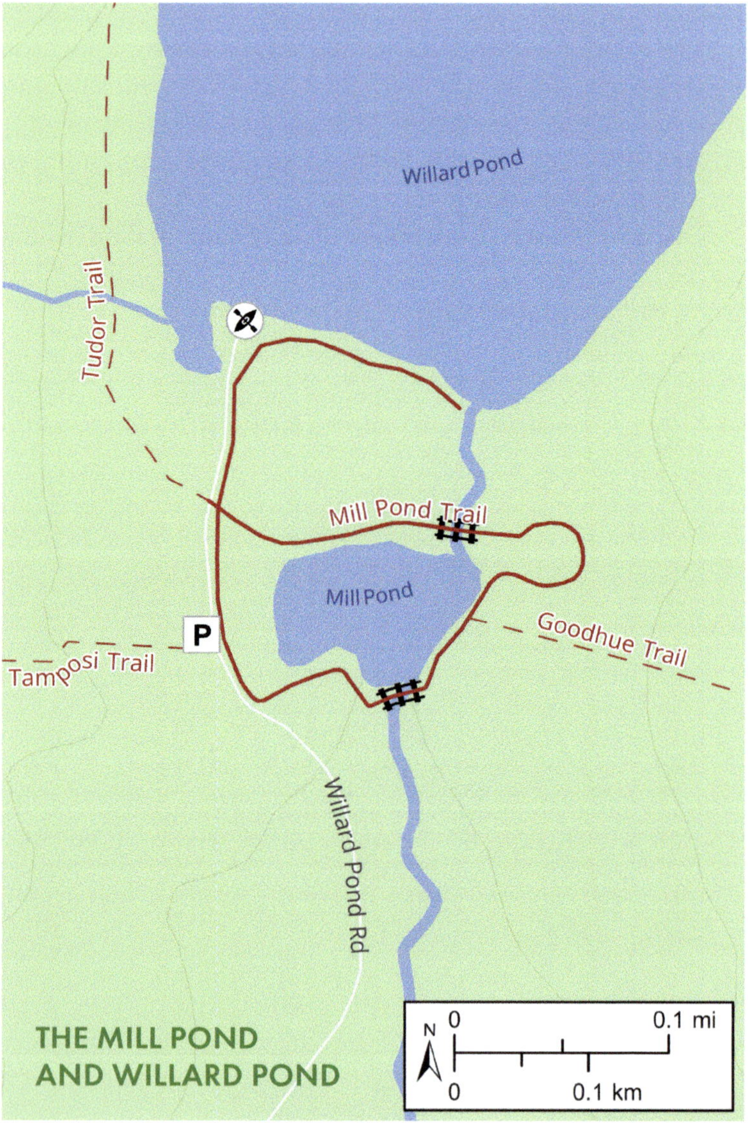
Willard Pond
Tudor Trail
Mill Pond Trail
Mill Pond
Goodhue Trail
P
Tamposi Trail
Willard Pond Rd
N
0
0.1 mi
0
0.1 km
THE MILL POND
AND WILLARD POND

Lay of the Land

TRAILS: One mile (round trip) for Mill Pond Trail and Willard Pond extension with some rocky terrain; several miles of other trails including Tudor, Tamposi, Bald Mountain, Goodhue Hill, Spur, and extended Mill Pond Trails

ACCESS: Large parking area on the left near the end of Willard Pond Road in Antrim

PERMITTED USES: Foot traffic only; dogs OK on a short leash on some trails

A GREAT PLACE TO: Introduce a friend to the region

INSIDER TIP: Bring a canoe or kayak to paddle Willard Pond after a hike

DON'T MISS: The balanced boulder near the parking lot

CREATURE FEATURE: Common loon

TREASURE HUNT: The stone engraving honoring Forbes Leland

FAVORITE MONTH: August

SNAPSHOT: Bald Mountain from the beaver dam

OWNERSHIP: New Hampshire Audubon

DIRECTIONS:

MicroExploring Practices

Micro Buddies

Exploring the beauty of nature is easier and more fun with a buddy. Sometimes friends meet just to chat and have a drink, but early on in our friendship, the two of us realized that we would rather *do* than talk. We found ourselves going on brief but meaningful nature expeditions every week. Sometimes we walked, sometimes we biked, and sometimes we paddled. There was never much planning, and that was part of the fun, not knowing on a given morning that we would end up watching the sunset from a canoe.

Sometimes it was just us, and sometimes we brought the kids, but it was always a pile of fun. The regularity of our trips was due not to obligation or routine but to the simple realization that in the course of each walk life would change from stressful to beautiful and peaceful. It wasn't a luxury; it was a necessity that helped balance our lives as humans, fathers, and friends.

More Than Just Company

When you bring a friend, low-level vigilance softens. You relax. You share the responsibility of staying safe, and with that comes a deeper sense of ease. Attention shifts—from survival mode to sensory mode. A buddy helps you get out of your own head. With two sets of eyes and ears, you catch more details—birdcalls, hidden fungi, the way the light flickers through the trees. You see more. Feel more. Remember more.

Together, you and a buddy can help motivate each other to go outside and find new places and ways to explore. When your buddy suggests an outing, say yes, sometimes even if you don't feel like it. You'll likely be glad you went. Contribute by bringing food, drinks, or essentials. Be ready by setting a meeting time and showing up prepared to maximize MicroExploration time and minimize idle time. Take turns leading. When your Micro buddy lacks energy, step in to plan and design the trip. Memories are the gold of life. Take photos and send them to each other at the end of the day.

Friendships are built on shared experiences. By MicroExploring the world together, you'll create lasting memories and strengthen your bonds with your environment, yourself, and each other.

Beautiful experiences in nature act as superglue, connecting friends and family.

CRANBERRY MEADOW POND 10
BEAT THE BUGS

Roadside Reset

Peterborough

It is not half so important to *know* as to *feel*.

—Rachel Carson

Walk Summary

Close to downtown Peterborough, a model for community-driven conservation has taken shape along a trail system that connects friends, neighbors, and strangers. Here, one can walk from paved streets into meadows, wetlands, and woodlands to a water source where cranberries grow wild.

Highlights

- Meander through a meadow in bloom
- Enjoy the sights and sounds of wetland birds from a boardwalk trail
- Meet friends and greet strangers along this trail that connects a community
- Reflect along a gentle woodland stream as you follow it to its secret source
- Climb the mountain that watches over Peterborough

The dream began in the mid-1980s when neighbors purchased twenty-three acres of pasture, the Cheney field, to prevent its development. They donated it to the town. Over the years, the town and the Monadnock Conservancy pieced together adjacent parcels—the Fernald, Kane, and Cranberry Meadow Pond conservation easements, all set aside for recreation and habitat protection.

In 2017, local forester Swift Corwin was inspired by a visit to an Italian village in the Alps where a trail led from a town to a mountaintop. He asked, "Why not here?" Working with the Peterborough Conservation Commission, he got support from private landowners, the town, and the Monadnock Conservancy to build a trail connecting the various ownerships, including lands not under conservation. The idea was that a community invested in the goal of bringing everyone into nature is a stronger one. In describing the process of trail building, Swift likened making trails to a form of public art. Today, the trail's popularity has surprised even its creators. You'll rarely find the parking lot empty.

Woodlands to Meadow

Enter the trail at the gate across from the kiosk on Old Street Road. Blue diamond markers lead you into the shade of tall hemlocks and pines. The main trail runs just a quarter mile here to the meadow, but you can lengthen it by taking the Wheeler Trail, which detours along and across a lovely brook.

A visit to the Cranberry Meadow Pond Trail may be about the namesake destination, but it doesn't have to be. The meadow might just be enough. Follow a meandering, single-track deer

path through a grassy field full of asters, goldenrod, and milkweed. A meadow has many configurations of color, texture, and feel that change with the seasons. Native plants are desirable in a landscape for ecological reasons, but the invaders have attractive features you have to admire—the green glow of buckthorn in the October sun, a jumble of bright-red and black berries on multiflora rose and autumn olive. Some people make a tart jam from the olives.

The path rises slowly to a crest, where you can get a view of Monadnock's summit just peeking above houses to the west. Then looking back behind you, you can see Pack Monadnock's dark spruce canopy and perhaps catch a glimpse of the rock face on North Pack. Birds sound off from snags and a cattail marsh near the Cheney Avenue trailhead at the field's far end. Bluebirds and tree swallows nest in boxes near apple trees, and bobolinks and American kestrels drop into the field in spring. The neighbors pitch in to mow the field annually in fall so birds and other wildlife can thrive.

Follow Water to Its Source: Cranberry Meadow Pond

In addition to providing easy access to often secluded places, boardwalks allow close observation of frogs, turtles, and wetland plants. Take this one slowly and remember to listen, if only to notice the sound of your own footfalls.

Backtracking to the trailhead on Old Street Road, begin your hike to Cranberry Meadow Pond along a trail maintained by the Monadnock Conservancy. This easy, one-mile walk follows a gentle stream to its source, the pond, and makes a fine out-and-back journey. An elevated boardwalk—one of few in the region—carries you across a wetland full of cattails, turtles, dragonflies, and birds. There's something about the sound of footfalls on wooden planks, and it's always an exciting feature for kids. In the summer, look for the yellow flowering stalks of swamp candles and in July, ripe blueberries. A platform allows for a small gathering, and it's a nice place to bring a chair. If you're still, you may see frogs rising to the surface, painted turtles on floating logs, or yellow warblers and flycatchers zipping from tree to tree.

Ahead, a private trail junction enters from the right just past a stone wall, and an old logging road crosses the trail (and brook), indicated by lush ferns and abundant saplings. Dappled sunlight shines through hemlock and hardwoods with an open

This thoughtfully designed trail dances along a meandering brook that leads to its wild source.

understory that eases the mind. The shallow brook flows gently and invites children to explore its banks and streambeds.

An older forest with big oaks and aspens reverts to a younger one on an abutting property. Many smaller trees, including those growing over the trail, are bent at wild angles, and some larger trees have snapped. The ice storm of 2008 left its mark here. Despite being cut and bent by ice, many of these young and flexible birches still survive. We can take a lesson from them!

Ice storms are powerful weather events that can leave their mark on the landscape. Trees break—or adapt—providing valuable lessons to us during stormy times of our own.

Cranberry Meadow Pond shimmers blue through the dense forest, and soon you're upon its edge. A viewpoint with primitive benches allows for a peaceful sit where floating bog mats, a beaver lodge, waterfowl, and a view of the Pack summit can be enjoyed. It's a fine spot to pull out a book and read, the tall pines providing shade and a whisper as you sit.

In the late 1800s, Granville Felt cultivated cranberries in the meadow, damming the pond. Harvested by hand, the cranberries were transported by train from Depot Square in Peterborough. You might not find cranberries here anymore (or you might if you venture forth into the marsh edge), but this trail is an excellent respite so close to downtown.

Beyond the Pond

If you want more, continue through hilly woods another 1.3 miles to East Mountain Road and a parking lot, which allows for a point-to-point hike. From here, a short connector trail leads to the Raymond Trail and its steep, 1.5-mile ascent of Pack Monadnock, where more adventures await.

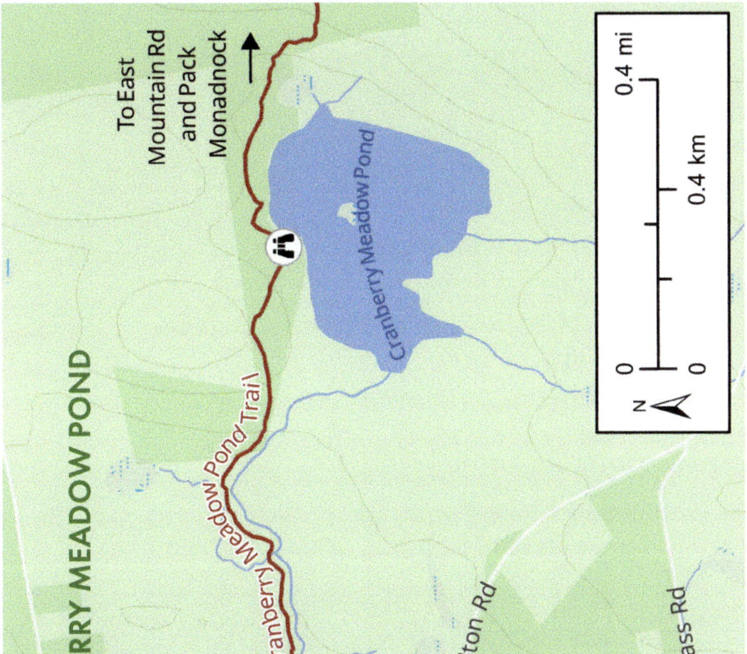
CRANBERRY MEADOW POND
To East Mountain Rd and Pack Monadnock
Cranberry Meadow Pond
Cranberry Meadow Pond Trail
Wilton Rd
Bass Rd
Old Street Rd
Cheney Ave
Wheeler Trail
P
0
0.4 mi
0.4 km
N

Lay of the Land

TRAILS: 1.5 miles of trails between meadow and pond of mostly gently rolling terrain; several miles of trails in total

ACCESS: Roadside parking along the east side of Old Street Road near Route 101/Wilton Road

PERMITTED USES: Foot traffic only; dogs OK on short leash at all times

A GREAT PLACE TO: Wade in a stream with a young explorer

INSIDER TIP: Connect all the way to Pack Monadnock for a longer hike

DON'T MISS: The meadow in bloom

CREATURE FEATURE: Monarch butterfly

TREASURE HUNT: Ice storm damage on a young hardwood forest

FAVORITE MONTH: December

SNAPSHOT: Pack Monadnock across the meadow

OWNERSHIP: Privately owned conservation easements held by Monadnock Conservancy and the Town of Peterborough

DIRECTIONS:

MicroExploring Practices

Beat the Bugs

In addition to its human conservation partners, the SuperSanctuary has another ally helping to keep its green spaces unspoiled: insects, including pesty ones! If you're out in nature in this part of the world, there's simply no way around it: you'll have to contend with the bugs. By late April, the swarms of blackflies descend, followed by mosquitoes, deer flies, and more. And of course there are the ticks. With a little bit of preparation, you can navigate these natural inconveniences and still enjoy the outdoors. Besides, they provide a natural balance to our surrounding ecosystems. Well, at least most of them do.

Don't let the bugs keep your family indoors when spring comes around! Defend yourself! Pulling your socks up over your pants seals off the main points of entry for ticks. Bug nets may not be ideal for a first date, but they are an essential gear item for keeping mosquitoes away from your face so you can enjoy nature in bug season.

Ticks

Ticks seem to be the exception. They emerge as soon as the snow begins to melt in March or April. Be aware of these arachnids in brushy edges, tall grass, and off-trail in the woodland understory. Dogs seem particularly good at attracting them, and they're easily passed along to us. Deer ticks, also called black-legged ticks, can carry Lyme and other diseases, so preventing their bites is especially important. You can spray your clothing and shoes with permethrin, which kills ticks on contact, or wear clothing pretreated with permethrin. Studies suggest a high level of effectiveness for both approaches. If you don't feel comfortable with a chemical option, there are natural tick repellents made from essential oils, which, if applied often, are also effective. Light-colored clothing helps with detection. Regardless of what you choose, check yourself often.

Blackflies and Mosquitoes

Blackflies and mosquitoes provide a one-two punch of swarming pests that might be enough to keep you indoors on what otherwise would be excellent conditions for wildlife viewing and outdoor exploration. Don't let them stop you! The blackflies come first, usually in late April, and are biting mainly between Mother's Day and Father's Day. Though they're not fast, their powers are in their numbers and persistence, and their bites can cause itchy reactions and welts in some. Mosquitoes typically emerge in May and persist in wet spells right through early fall, most common around wetlands. Repellents will work to some degree, but a bug net, loose-fitting light-colored clothing, and long sleeves are recommended.

Deer flies

By July, when mosquitoes begin to die down, deer flies emerge. The ninjas of the insect world, they will congregate and swarm around your head, exposed skin, and even bite through clothing. Keep them at bay by dressing in light colors and covering your head and neck; a wide-brimmed hat completes the outfit. You can also turn your hat into a deer fly trap with duct tape and some Tanglefoot goo; you'll amass quite a collection by the end of your hike!

Yellowjackets

By July and August, nesting yellowjackets and hornets are a possibility along your favorite trails. Staying vigilant will help, and if you do come across a ground nest, do your best to mark its location, and be sure to pass along that information to the trail manager. In some cases, a temporary reroute will allow other hikers to continue using the trail safely.

If You Can't Beat 'Em . . .

You can always opt to enjoy nature another way. Kayaking or canoeing on an open pond or lake will reduce your encounters with flying insect pests, and biking is another great option (if you can keep ahead of the swarms!). Plus there's always the scenic Micro drive.

A lovely paddle can be an excellent way to enjoy the outdoors in bug season.

LOVERENS MILL CEDAR SWAMP
THE GREEN CHURCH 11

Wilderness Preserved

Antrim, Stoddard, and Windsor

In every walk with Nature one receives far more than he seeks.

—John Muir

Walk Summary

A visit to the Loverens Mill Cedar Swamp Preserve transcends generations, even millennia. It reveals ancient forests full of large boulders and diverse wetlands. At its heart is a fifty-acre Atlantic white cedar swamp—the Granite State's second largest. Immerse yourself in the silence of a winter conifer forest or the cacophony of a cascading river, and witness old and new technologies harnessing the energy of nature.

Highlights

- **Experience the sound of silence amid rare Atlantic white cedars**
- **Enjoy the feel of a cool northern forest in summer**
- **Visit a unique natural community with rare plant species**
- **Explore massive boulders and glacial formations like eskers and bogs**
- **Admire how water and wind energy were harnessed in different eras**
- **Reconcile the concept of wilderness next to a highway and mills**

Park at a small parking lot just across the North Branch of the Contoocook River on Loverens Mill Road; the lot is owned and maintained by New Hampshire Fish and Game. A kiosk here hosts a sign that describes the history and ecology of the preserve. A short walk north along the road will bring you to a sign that points left past a green gate toward the preserve.

Few places have the feel of a cedar swamp. Near the northern edge of its range, Loverens Mill Cedar Swamp Preserve harbors one of the state's last remaining populations of Atlantic white cedar—a species once widespread, now surviving only in protected pockets. But this preserve protects more than just rare

A spring walk here is full of blooms (clockwise, from top left: painted trillium, swamp azalea, hobblebush, red trillium).

trees. A wide variety of wetland and upland plants and excellent wildlife habitat remains under the capable stewardship of one of the world's conservation leaders, the Nature Conservancy (TNC).

Close to the sounds of the highway, surrounded by history and abundant plant and animal life, you might ponder if you're truly alone here. Perhaps you sense the dichotomy of being in such an ancient, wild forest so close to a main highway. Would you know the highway was there if you couldn't hear its distant hum?

Before stepping through the gate, glance up the road toward the wind turbines on Tuttle Hill. This may be your only clear view if the trees are leafed out. Then begin the walk along a grassy single-track trail through a diverse hardwood forest owned and managed by Meadowsend Consulting Company, a conservation partner. Painted trilliums and Canada mayflowers bloom trailside, while basswoods, elms, and cherry trees arch overhead.

The sound of the nearby highway is soon drowned out by the rushing waters of the North Branch River, a major tributary of the Contoocook. Just a few steps off the main trail to the left, a short spur brings you to a roaring stretch of river—an unexpected cascade for a region better known for quiet streams. The SuperSanctuary lacks the tall waterfalls of the White Mountains or northern Vermont, but its rivers can carry an impressive volume of water.

The trail broadens into an old woods road lined with oaks, and a short climb leads to a viewpoint of more falls and the remnants of Loveren's Mill. A concrete dam foundation and granite blocks mark the spot where Josiah Loveren expanded a 1798 sawmill and gristmill into a bustling hub producing cedar shingles, timber, and siding for the developing town of Antrim. Later in the mill's history, the Batchelder family manufactured cable reels, crib dowels, and small boxes that held the sound mechanism for the once-popular "Mama" dolls. The mill closed in the 1920s, but its energy source, flowing water, has a successor. On the ridge above, tall wind turbines harness a modern renewable force. What might come next?

In contrast to the rapids below, the water above the dam is calm and flat. Brook trout hide in the pools, and otters, herons, and kingfishers fish for them. You can, too, or just sit for a bit and watch. Let the noise of your own thoughts be drowned out by the river's relentless sound.

The raging North Branch of the Contoocook rushes with whitewater during spring's melt-off.

The Preserve: A Sea of Green

When continuing, you'll see a small sign indicating that you've entered the 1,200-acre TNC preserve. A shallow but wide pit on the left side of the trail fills up with water in the spring. Its squarish shape suggests it was human-made, but what exactly was it for? This spot offers ridgeline views when the trees are leafless or fine fall foliage viewing. Enter the TNC trail system at a signed ninety-degree right turn, pause at the small trailhead kiosk, use the boot brush to prevent the spread of invasive seeds, and then hike on!

The preserve is dressed with evergreens from floor to ceiling. Wintergreen and partridgeberry carpet the forest floor, each with its distinctive tiny leaves and berries, interspersed with bunchberry, trailing arbutus (whose small white flowers appear in early spring), pockets of bluebead lily (bearing yellow flowers in spring), and pink lady's slippers. Fir, spruce, and hemlock saplings crowd the understory—get tactile to differentiate the "spiky spruce" from the "friendly fir." Above are older spruces and white pines. Hardwood trees are less common here but include red maples and paper (white) birches.

A short side trail to the right leads to one of the coolest places on the property—a cavernous rock pile that allows exploration of its fascinating interior space. Growing on and amid the stones, you'll see arcs of rock polypody (a type of fern) and patches of brown-and-black rock tripe (a kind of lichen). Take notice of where each grows best on these broken rocks, and wonder why. This pile of boulders is kid-tested and safe for parents, too!

Cedars and Big Boulders

Just a half mile from the trailhead, the Cedar View Trail veers right. If your goal is to stand among cedars, this is the trail to follow. This short spur leads into one of the rarest forest types in New England, a fifty-two-acre Atlantic white cedar swamp. (Only a few hundred acres exist in the whole state.) This cedar, a southern species, grows here in a northern forest at the highest and most inland location in the state. Cedars stand close together, their bark growing in long reddish strips, their limbs short and curling. Notice how their narrow crowns lean, perhaps shaped by wind, and listen to them creak with wind. Pollen core records indicate this forest has been growing for four thousand years, and some trees are upward of 130 years old.

Cedar swamps are some of the rarest habitats remaining in New England. Let your senses lead you along the short boardwalk through the cedars.

Two hundred feet of creaky bog bridges lead you through the cedar swamp; it's like entering a different world, marked by mossy bog mats and wetland shrubs. Bogs and other wetlands have long been known as sacred places for medicinal plants and other botanical necessities; it's likely that Abenaki peoples gathered plants here. Labrador tea plants (a type of rhododendron), creeping snowberry (ground vines with short, round leaves and white fruit), and yellow loosestrife grow among the sphagnum moss mat of the bog. The rare swamp azalea grows here, too, producing fragrant pink flowers in spring, while fall foliage here is spectacular, highlighted by yellow ferns and red shrubs contrasting with the evergreen cedars.

The "giant with an underbite."

Get down low with the little things in here. Use a hand lens or turn your binoculars upside down. Look at the sphagnum moss up close and notice its shape. Keep your ears open, too. Breeding bird diversity is similar to sites much farther north: Canada and Nashville warblers, northern waterthrushes, and rarely, a rusty blackbird.

This trail terminates in a small diamond of bog bridges. Take a moment to tune in to your senses. How do you feel here? Calm? Protected? Sacred? The remainder of the trail system is worth further exploration if you have the time. With the cedar swamp on your right, the trail leads past a series of surprises: two cabin-size boulders followed by an even larger one, barely visible through the hemlocks—a hulking erratic, cracked open, now sheltering a growing hemlock in its fracture. It's the kind of rock you could imagine being named "the giant with an underbite."

The Loop Trail and Lookout Point

Almost a mile into the trail system, the loop begins, and we often go right—perhaps because our ears guide us away from the traffic of Route 9. The right loop skirts the continuing cedar and spruce wetland, which is surrounded by a moat of wetland shrubs, mainly mountain holly. The topography of the surrounding hills and basin funnels and retains cold air, resulting in northern plant life and wildlife, cooler temperatures, and a generally more northern feel. Along with the conifer canopy, the cooler air makes this route a choice hike on a hot summer day.

The path dips and winds through rocky, shaded forest. A patch of forest on the left features dying paper birches dropping out of the hemlock overstory, suggesting that they grew from a fire—or another significant canopy disturbance—many decades prior. Ironically, a warming climate now threatens the species' persistence in northern New England. You'll travel along elevated spines of the land called eskers, narrow ridges shaped by glacial meltwater. Red maples and hemlocks dominate here, their spacing wide, the light filtered. The trail dips, winds, ascends, and again showcases lowland cedars and spruces, just out of reach.

Tracking is a favorite winter activity here. Black bear sign is frequently encountered in this wild, protected landscape. Look for tracks of this omnivore in the shoulder seasons or on snow during mild winters.

Don't miss the short spur trail to Lookout Point. At its end, a Leopold bench sits amid leatherleaf and winterberry shrubs, with a backdrop of distant hills. With sounds of birds, frogs, and a trickling stream, this is a place to bask in wildness. Winterberry's spring leaves burst forth like tiny yellow candles. Otter and beaver signs are abundant here, and black bear tracks—occasionally accompanied by the real thing—can be observed in any season. If you're patient, or lucky, you may glimpse one at the wetland edge. Gaze northward across low, gentle hills from this intimate viewpoint.

The final leg winds through more of the preserve's quiet complexity of varied forest types, undulating terrain, boulders, and wetland landscapes. Open water wetlands appear intermittently. A beaver tail-slap may break the stillness, or perhaps the drumming of a ruffed grouse. Hobblebush blooms in early May along the river, the white of its blossoms matching the whitewater it grows near. Its multicolored leaves stun in the fall.

The return trip, as you pass many of these same features again, is like a little farewell. Promise them a return again soon. A visit to Loverens Mill may gift you with a sense of wildness and complexity just off the beaten path.

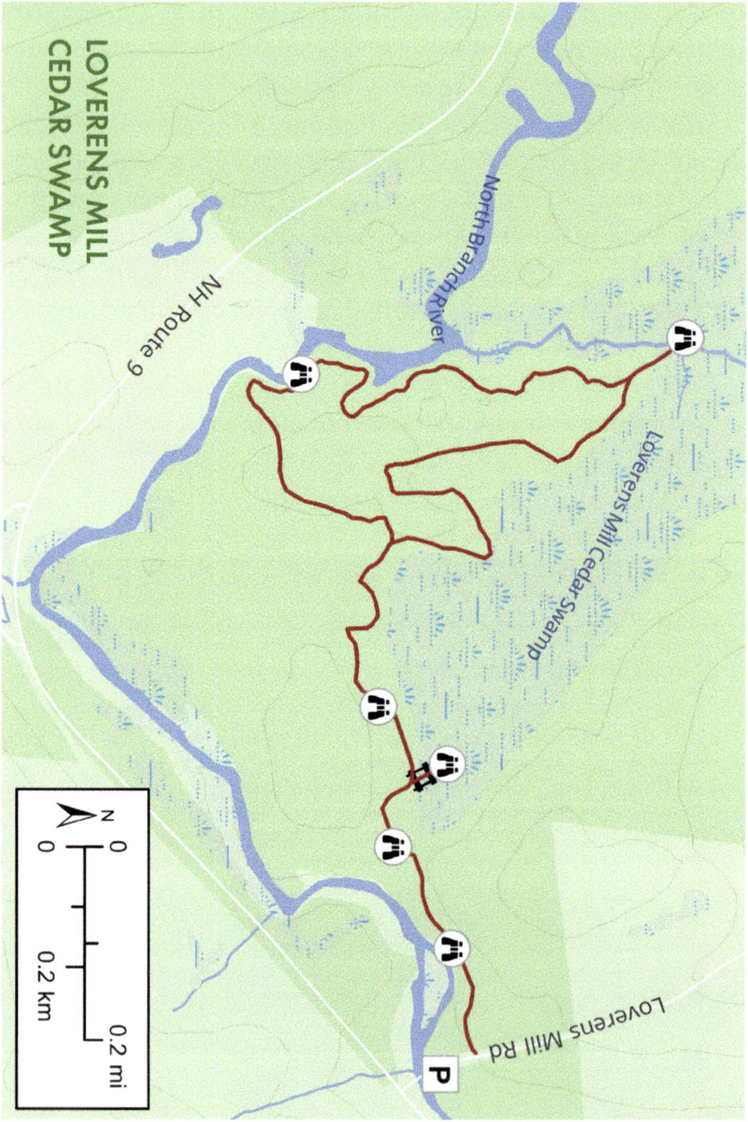
LOVERENS MILL
CEDAR SWAMP
North Branch River
NH Route 9
Loverens Mill Cedar Swamp
Loverens Mill Rd
P
N
0
0
0.2 mi
0.2 km

Lay of the Land

TRAILS: Three-mile loop trail over mostly gently rolling terrain; marked by green and yellow square markers

ACCESS: Parking area on Loverens Mill Road off Route 9 between Hillsborough and Stoddard

PERMITTED USES: Foot traffic only; no pets

A GREAT PLACE TO: Experience a rare plant community

INSIDER TIP: Combine a walk here with a fishing trip on the North Branch River

DON'T MISS: The rare experience of being in a cedar forest—the feel of the trees' bark, the creaking of their twisted trunks

CREATURE FEATURE: Black bear

TREASURE HUNT: The gigantic glacial boulder just off the trail

FAVORITE MONTH: January

SNAPSHOT: Rushing water through the old mill

OWNERSHIP: The Nature Conservancy, with smaller parcels protected by the Forest Society, Meadowsend Timberlands, New Hampshire Department of Transportation, and New Hampshire Fish and Game

DIRECTIONS:

MicroExploring Practices

The Green Church

Many of us grew up thinking church was a building. But for MicroExplorers, the green church is outside—wild, sacred, and alive with a power that's quiet, magical, and deeply felt. Our connection to nature's "church" is always within reach. Sometimes it's just beyond our doorstep—at the edge of a trail, down a quiet stretch of river, or tucked into a familiar patch of woods. But the deeper entrance—the one that changes us—is inward. To walk into the living world and actually arrive is an act not just of movement but also of presence.

The Practice of Presence

Nature can touch our soul—but only if we're open enough to let it in. For minds that are often navigating the complexities of modern life, including anxieties, disconnection, and distraction, learning to fully feel and absorb the natural world is not as easy as it seems. It's a practice, somewhat of a lost art. It's a Jedi mental exercise that must be consciously carried out, observed, and relearned. If your body is in the woods but your mind is somewhere else, you may be walking right past the healing that was waiting for you. We must be conscious of how we are breathing, what we are hearing and feeling, and where our emotional state of mind is trying to take us so we can rein it back to peace.

The Mind Untangled

Exploring the complex beauty of the natural environment makes it much harder for your brain to loop itself back into shallow thinking. The patterns in trees, branches, and bark, as well as the multitudinous fractals, shapes, and colors you encounter, disrupt rigid thought processes, acting as a powerful antidote to the mind's constant efforts to categorize and label its surroundings. They cool off the mind's engine before it overheats.

True intelligence is being comfortable with the idea that the answers to our most fundamental questions—where we came from, where we are supposed to go, and how we are supposed to live our lives—are all already out there, in nature. That magical power has been alive in plants, animals, and all living beings since the beginning of life. Life itself knows, but that information is not written in English—it's encoded inside the memories of our bodies. To connect to that language, that intelligence, we must go beyond our brains and go deep inside our very instincts.

Enter nature as you would a temple, and it will bless you with peace and a deepened connection to yourself.

Trees as Healers

On days when we walk in nature feeling heavy and down, we can feel the trees drawing stagnant negative energy away from us. The wooden colossi give us both perspective and protection. We may feel a little guilty leaving all that behind, as if we've littered the forest with our darkness, until we begin to understand that nature has a way of creating balance in itself. Just as trees take in the carbon dioxide we exhale, they also seem to absorb our sadness, our anxiety, our worries, leaving us lighter, clearer, and renewed. The quiet of the forest is not a vacuum; it is the language of nature.

Create shared adventures in nature with children. Show them that the world is bigger than a screen. By teaching them to love the forest, you are building a sanctuary in their soul that they can return to whenever the storms of life roll in.

Listening to the Language

The sound of wind through the canopy, the crinkle of leaves beneath our feet, the delicate songs of birds—each carries a message. Attune yourself to the gentle narratives that nature is trying to whisper to you. Is it trying to soothe you and calm you down? Is it reminding you that everything is going to be OK? The language of nature goes beyond human words, so connecting to what you hear is an exercise in remaining present, elevating your mind out of its muck, and reconnecting to your body and your senses.

The Science of Trees

Studies have shown that spending time in nature, including forests with trees, provides a calming environment that signals to our bodies that we are safe and can relax. Levels of cortisol, the body's primary stress hormone, decrease, which can help slow the heart rate and lower blood pressure. Trees also release organic compounds called phytoncides into the air; research suggests that inhaling these compounds can boost our immune system. The sheltering presence of trees can evoke a feeling of being protected and cared for by the natural world, which can be emotionally soothing. Make sure to hug a tree, rest on a log, and touch the leaves on the branches as you walk.

HIROSHI LOOP 12
TRAILSIDE TREATS

Tranquil Loop
Peterborough, Harrisville, and Dublin

There is one main path, a loop, but a hundred ways you could go.

—Alice B. Fogel

Walk Summary

Not far from several town centers, the Hiroshi Loop Trail follows a river, takes in mountain views, and traverses a beautiful array of wildlife habitats. It is gentle but provides enough challenge for those looking for more than a stroll. The parking lot and surrounding meadow are destinations themselves, and the lovely loop is one to enjoy slowly and in all seasons. It is a trail that invites the user to slow down and observe the changes and the constants, tucked away in distance and time.

Highlights

- Repeat this hike: inviting and easy-going, it's the kind of trail you can return to over and over
- Observe different wetland types and habitats throughout the walk
- Ideal for a slow walk in thoughtful solitude
- Look for spring ephemeral wildflowers
- Bathe in the warm winter light along a placid brook
- Listen for thrushes and warblers singing in spring and summer

Conveniently close to Hancock, Dublin, Harrisville, Peterborough, and Jaffrey, Hiroshi is a nearby getaway. The pleasure begins the moment you arrive. Despite the surrounding woodlands, the parking area always seems to bask in sunshine on clear days. In the spring, it is filled with lively birdsong; in summer, the surrounding fields glow; in fall, the foliage beckons; and in winter, the silence of snowfall is majestic.

The fields and associated open paths are mowed late in summer and bloom with grasses and wildflowers, buzzing with pollinators by day and fireflies by night. A sentinel sugar maple, now in decline, still commands attention in the field to the south, and radiant white paper birches dot the wood line to the north. In spring, admire the flowering apple trees next to the old homestead, now just a granite foundation.

Hayashi Hiroshi owned the property prior to its conservation by the Harris Center. He also owned a local restaurant in Peterborough and operated the Monadnock School for Natural Cooking and Philosophy at a former center here.

The Hiroshi trailhead and surrounding meadow is a destination on its own.
Photo by Chuck Carlson

Whether you visit alone or with friends, the trailhead bench next to the simple wooden kiosk suggests a mindful approach to this walk. Beaver-chewed walking sticks for borrowing often lean against the kiosk. Grab one; you won't regret it. Look up to observe the wide-branching ash trees, now starkly bare even in summer due to the emerald ash borer, an invasive insect. Behind the kiosk lies the foundation of an old barn and a double stone wall (a former livestock run) that marks the beginning of the loop trail. When you've basked long enough in the open, head downhill.

The large parking area is plowed in winter and makes a good meeting place for small groups.

The trail—an old road for a time—makes its steepest descent through a wet hardwood forest rich in plant diversity. After a hard left into young hemlocks, hints of a wetland appear on the left. During spring, peepers and red-winged blackbirds may be audible, or you may simply notice the distant opening where light gathers. The first of several pairs of cut stumps invites hikers to sit and enjoy some of the more than one hundred species of birds that have been recorded on the property. Listen for broad-winged hawks, scarlet tanagers, swamp sparrows, hermit thrushes, and more. Just ahead, you'll have to make the hardest decision of the walk—right or left at the fork?

Beginning the Loop

Whether you choose by the sun, the wind, or simply which way your walking stick guides you, you can't go wrong. Heading left will take you into a section of the loop signed IN FINE FEATHER, where a Harris Center project pairs music with hiking. A right here keeps you out of direct northwest winds, which often prevail in winter.

If you go left, this lovely stretch of trail dances along the wetland edge. A few careful steps toward the wetland may give you a fine vantage point for wildlife viewing or basking in afternoon sunshine. Pause only briefly here, as other wetland views lie ahead, all worthwhile. After a short distance, the path climbs gradually and enters a more wooded area through mixed forests.

Eventually, a descent into a darker hemlock hollow gives way to an area of dense understory vegetation, where logging from a decade earlier reallocated light to the forest floor. The axe may fall here again, as active management is one chosen path to steward forests. No forest is stagnant; there will be change, whether by selective cutting, fire, or invasive insect.

A large boulder on the right marks the start of heavy beaver activity. Wide swaths of barren ground—beaver trails—crisscross the now single-file footpath. The old red oaks here first grew before beavers inhabited the area and must now contend with these herbivores. But oaks are survivors, with a little help from us. Here the Harris Center prevents beavers from girdling these massive trail trees by applying mesh fencing around their trunks. Blue boundary markers, signs being swallowed by trees, and occasional metal pipes mark the edge of the floodplain and abutting property owned by the Army Corps of Engineers. This area is protected for flood control purposes to prevent such natural disasters as the Great Flood of 1936, which inundated downtown Peterborough (and much of the Northeast) and led to the passage of the Flood Control Act of 1936.

Dinsmore Pond and Nubanusit Brook

The placid view of wild Dinsmore Pond is an unexpected reward, one worthy of a photograph, a painting, or at least a few minutes of admiration. Look out to Thumb and Skatutakee Mountains near the headwaters. This pond is the only one dammed solely by beavers (rather than humans) along this great brook's fourteen-mile length. Its natural shoreline habitat includes riparian forest and a less common floating bog mat, full of black spruce, tamarack, and leatherleaf shrubs, which give off a reddish hue in leaf-off season.

Follow your ears to the sound of flowing water where the pond's outlet narrows into Nubanusit Brook, which flows in all but the coldest winter conditions. Below the tall pines, you may notice small, broad-leaved evergreens. Sheep laurel and leatherleaf retain their leaves in winter. Leatherleaf's small, white, bell-like flowers are favored by early pollinators in early May, while sheep laurel's clusters of pink flowers appear in late June. Look closely at the forest floor, and you'll see dense mats of winterberry, which has short, round leaves and bright-red berries. Both the berries and the leaves make a minty trailside snack. Follow your nose to the trailing arbutus, or mayflower, whose sweet-smelling, pinkish flowers bloom now in late April (rather than May, for which they were named) under larger oval leaves.

Abundant water views dominate for the next quarter mile as the trail remains quite narrow. Slow down here for the best chances of sighting wildlife such as beavers, minks, otters, and abundant frogs and newts on a humid summer morning.

Across the brook are trails used for many years by the Sargent Camp, a former summer camp. A clearing along the bank is a fine place to pause and watch the shallow river flow. Here, campers used a raft and pulley to cross the water. Look for remaining evidence of this infrastructure in the trees on either side. Ahead, the bank steepens, leading to beaver-browsed shrubs and pointy stumps—blond in the case of the recently chewed, black for the older. At the end of this stretch, the brook meanders through a broad valley and veers away from the trail, leaving hikers feeling that there is more—an essential Micro experience. Because there always is.

A young MicroExplorer proudly holds a ribbon snake found along the trail before returning it to the wild.

Follow the winding trail along the brook, passing a vernal pool on the right. Tall pines tower overhead, their green tips glowing yellow in the fading evening light of a summer day. Shoreline trees limit views in all but a few treasured locations of the trail, where the river looks different at each viewpoint. There is good silence on this stretch, especially in winter. Eventually, the trail jogs away from the brook for good and returns through a hemlock forest to that first junction.

Now, what would this walk have been like if you had followed the sign reading THE SINGING STREAM to the right? Maybe next time you'll find out!

Follow the sun on a "one-hour wonder."

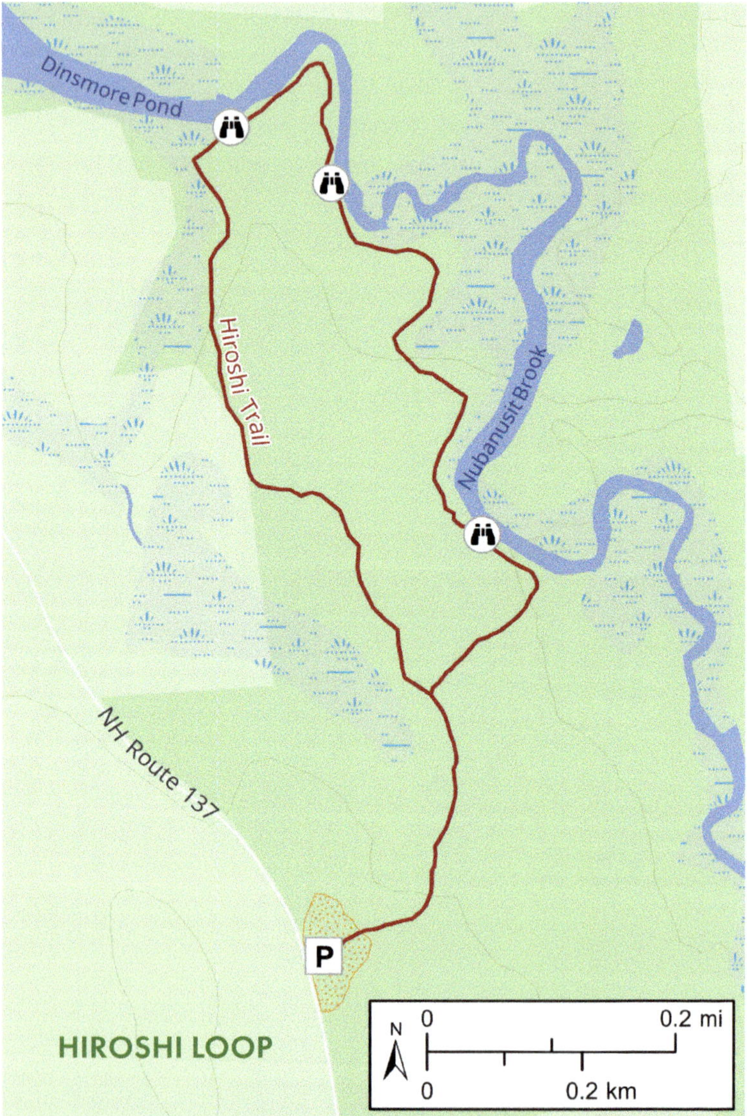
Dinsmore Pond
Hiroshi Trail
Nubanusit Brook
NH Route 137
P
HIROSHI LOOP
N
0
0.2 mi
0
0.2 km

Lay of the Land

TRAILS: 1.9-mile Hiroshi Loop Trail traverses mostly gently rolling terrain with some roots and rocky sections

ACCESS: Parking area (plowed in winter) off Harrisville Road near the Dublin/Harrisville town line

PERMITTED USES: Foot traffic only; dogs OK on short leash at all times

A GREAT PLACE TO: Take a silent winter stroll

INSIDER TIP: Walk it clockwise one time, counterclockwise the next

DON'T MISS: The flood control markers from 1976 sunk into the ground

CREATURE FEATURE: Beaver

TREASURE HUNT: The remains of the pulley raft across Nubanusit Brook

FAVORITE MONTH: March

SNAPSHOT: Dinsmore Pond view

OWNERSHIP: Harris Center for Conservation Education

DIRECTIONS:

MicroExploring Practices

Trailside Treats

The anticipation of a refreshing escape into nature often clashes with the contents of our hiking bags. Ingrained habits make people pack the predictable: granola bar, apple, peanut butter and jelly, and a medley of old nuts.

In MicroExploring, we don't suffer the pain of plain! For us, food transcends mere sustenance; it's a heightened sensory experience that creates powerful memories and feelings of well-being. Elevating your outdoor culinary game isn't a luxury; it's an important way to engage with the world around you!

Everything tastes better outside. It's a fact. There's something special about a meal in nature. You're outside, which is fun, but it's also nourishment and a reward. When you've been walking an hour or two and you stop to eat, your body immediately welcomes the energy, and you feel relief and pleasure—your food serves as more than just sustenance.

From Rations to Rituals

Challenge yourself to level up the quality, quantity, and diversity of food and beverages you bring to your outdoor adventures. Forget survival rations—this is a picnic for your soul. Picture yourself under the shade of a tree on top of a mountain. You've been walking for an hour, and now you've conquered this beautiful mountain view. You indulge freshly baked gourmet croissant sandwiches filled with prosciutto and fig jam, or

The only thing better than fresh forest air is the smell of warm pastries wafting through it.

roasted vegetables with goat cheese and pesto, along with some Brazil and macadamia nuts. For a touch of sweetness, you've brought a selection of high-quality dark chocolates and delicate mini fruit tarts. To quench your thirst, you brought a fancy elderflower bubbly drink. And don't forget to connect to each season by tasting local food, fruits, and veggies produced locally in your region.

Eating amazing food out in nature creates a vivid, strong visual memory that your conscious and subconscious won't easily forget. When you're out shopping for food, consider selecting a few special items exclusively for your MicroExplorations.

Be daring and try things you normally wouldn't choose. Those special treats sitting in your fridge or pantry will serve as a reminder that you have an upcoming date with yourself and nature. If you have a Micro buddy, trying to outdo and surprise each other with unique food, snacks, and drinks is a playful way to add joy and anticipation to the journey.

Fuel for Body and Mood

Eating while you are out in nature isn't just about hunger; it's vital for regulating blood sugar, which prevents energy crashes, irritability, and loss of focus, helping you maintain a positive and even-keeled mood. Consistent fuel sustains you physically, keeps you feeling strong and in control, and allows you to tackle the trail with confidence. Indulge and explore!

SKATUTAKEE AND THUMB MOUNTAINS 13

LAUGHTER

Invigorating Views
Hancock

For a time I rest in the grace of the world, and am free.

—Wendell Berry

Hike Summary

At the heart of the Harris Center's expansive mosaic of conserved lands are the twin summits of Skatutakee and Thumb Mountains. Each one tops out just below two thousand feet in elevation and offers its own distinct, rich experience. They can be taken separately for shorter out-and-back hikes or combined for a lengthier loop, a true joyful journey.

Highlights

- Take in two summits with spectacular ridgeline and mountain views
- Invoke the feeling of a White Mountains experience closer to home
- Get to know a forever wild forest and its unique trees
- Discover the magic of a forest alive with realistic trailside animal carvings
- Search for insects and amphibians along the shores of a pristine pond
- Bask in a million-dollar view of Monadnock from Thumb Mountain

Before or after the Harris Center's extensive system of trails lures you in, make sure to check out the accessible grounds, pollinator garden, bird feeders, and new outdoor lodge. Perhaps pop into the center where naturalists, conservationists, and educators have poured their energies for over fifty years.

The Harris Center's bobcat weathervane shows the way.

Start out at the trailhead directly across the entrance from the Harris Center, the gateway to the West Side Trails. This first stretch of the Harriskat Trail descends briefly, crosses Kings Highway, and begins an ascent that is a good indication of the grade on the steeper parts of this trail farther along. Stay vigilant for owls, frogs, salamanders, and snakes—all presented trailside as larger-than-life, *in situ* carvings, the work of local volunteer and wood carver Jack McWhorter. The sinuous snake carved out of a fallen spruce is perfectly situated at eye level for the youngest hikers. This trail hosts live critters, too—keep an eye out for wood frogs and red-spotted newts. The wood frogs sound off from vernal pools near the carvings in early spring.

The great horned owl carving by Jack McWhorter.

Just half a mile in, this lovely trail through old oak and pine forests reaches a favorite destination for some, the forest floor cleared of debris where campers make forts. Continue up the Harriskat Trail, bearing left at the first junction toward Skatutakee's summit. Climbing steadily, the 1.5-mile uphill trail soon transitions into classic northern hardwood forest. Look for large legacy trees—American beech, yellow birch, sugar maple, and white ash—their rough bark revealing their advanced age. A particular red oak along a stone wall up high has lost its lower branches, either because they receive less sunlight or as a way to conserve the tree's energy. This "stayin' alive" tree is just one visible example of how the landscape shapes us all to some degree. Higher up, sentinel red spruces appear, eventually giving way to a spruce-dominated canopy and signaling proximity to the summit. Despite only half the elevation of a four-thousand-footer in the White Mountains, the feel is strikingly similar.

Bask in the shade of the spruce canopy, listen to the breeze blow through it, and breathe deeply to savor the trees' sweet fragrance.

There's more to admire than just trees. Glacial boulders, large and small, dot the forest floor, and a boulder train crosses the trail at the one-mile mark, where mountain maples grow and black-throated blue warblers sing their buzzy "*I-am-so-la-zy*" songs. Stone walls tell of a time when sheep pasture dominated even the higher terrain. Old blueberry bushes, thick mats of juniper, and an open-growing pasture tree or two are the only other evidence of those bygone days. Despite the forces of nature reclaiming the land, we still long for these open summit views. Trail crews from the Harris Center and occasionally the Student Conservation Association work hard to keep the paths clear and the views open.

Skatutakee's Summit

From the domed summit of Skatutakee, Pack Monadnock and North Pack lay themselves out prominently to the east (right to left), and Crotched Mountain looms farther north. A narrow view cut, maintained by volunteers, showcases Hancock's Norway Pond and the tall, defining steeple on Main Street. Take a picnic lunch on one of the small ledge outcrops, or perhaps save it for Thumb Mountain. For decades, Harris Center educators have taken school groups here to witness hawk migration, pick wild blueberries, and explore the rocky ledges. Many kids have wielded their first pair of binoculars or had their first foray "ponding" on these trails.

From Skatutakee's summit, follow the Thumbs Up Trail to the second of the twin peaks. This mile-long ridgeline is one of the most delightful high-elevation hikes in the region. The trail dives into an expansive spruce forest that is cool, quiet, and aromatic. Listen to the sound of spruce boughs diffusing the breeze through their fine needles. It's a sound that can't be replicated by any other tree.

Slope, soil types, and management history all influence forest composition, and the diversity along this ridge keeps the hike interesting. Watch the transitions as you walk. Carpets of club mosses give way to patches of ferns, then to a small swamp dominated by buttonbush shrubs nestled just below the next ascent.

Thumb Mountain: Big Rewards

At the T junction, bear left onto a short but steep ascent of Thumb Mountain. Behold the reward from a south-facing outcrop that looks out over half the SuperSanctuary to Mount Monadnock, which, from this angle, resembles a sleeping dragon. This view features an emerald triangle of green space between Monadnock, the Wapack Range, and you. A small plaque here bears a celebrated Thoreau quote, its pertinent reminder of simplicity something that we always find worth pondering as we bask here, resting and refueling.

The return via the Thumbs Down Trail is as interesting as the approach and traverses mixed forest types as it works its way back to the Harriskat Trail. One of the most peaceful spots along the way is Jack's Pond, a small, shallow pond surrounded by mossy stones and home to a wide variety of salamanders, frogs, and invertebrates. Depending on the season, you might hear wood frogs calling or spot dragonflies skimming the surface.

Jack's Pond is a fun surprise along this wooded route. It welcomes the MicroExplorer to search its edges for salamanders and frogs and also invites a peaceful rest.

Returning to where you started at the Harris Center, reflect on the journey you just took. Even if you only went as far as appreciating the wood carvings today, you've accomplished something important, essential to your health. You connected with some wildness, invoked your inner child, and experienced awe. Magic looms large in these forests, and it will seep into your subconscious if you practice receiving its gifts. Whether you come for foliage, wildlife, exercise, or the joy of walking under spruce trees, these twin summits will hold the answer. They're proof that you don't need to go far or high to feel wonder.

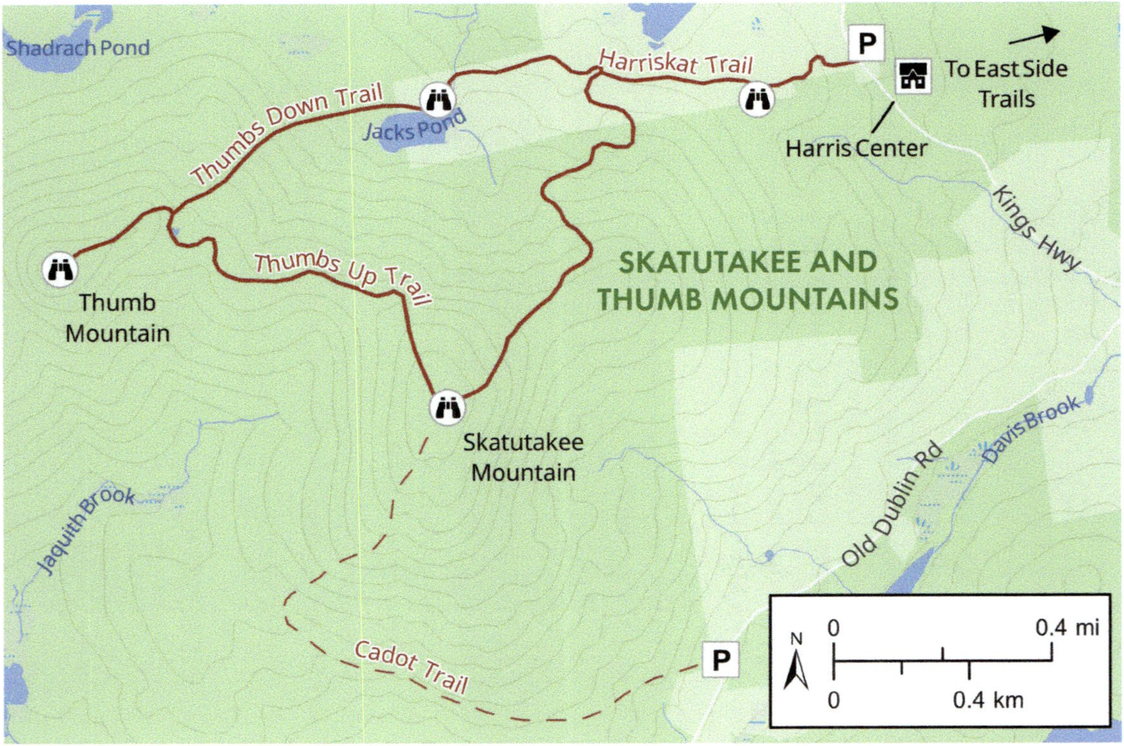
SKATUTAKEE AND THUMB MOUNTAINS
Shadrach Pond
Thumbs Down Trail
Jacks Pond
Harriskat Trail
P
To East Side Trails
Harris Center
Kings Hwy
Thumbs Up Trail
Thumb Mountain
Skatutakee Mountain
Jaquith Brook
Old Dublin Rd
Davis Brook
Cadot Trail
P
N
0
0.4 mi
0
0.4 km

Lay of the Land

TRAILS: 4.5-mile loop includes Harriskat, Thumbs Up, and Thumbs Down Trails; moderately steep terrain over a lengthy distance

ACCESS: Parking at the Harris Center for Conservation Education on Kings Highway

PERMITTED USES: Foot traffic only; dogs OK on short leash at all times

A GREAT PLACE TO: Listen to the wind in a spruce forest

INSIDER TIP: Bring a celebratory picnic to enjoy on one of the summits

DON'T MISS: The snake, frog, salamander, and owl carvings along the trail

CREATURE FEATURE: Wood frog

TREASURE HUNT: The quotation from Henry David Thoreau inscribed on a plaque at Thumb Mountain

FAVORITE MONTH: October

SNAPSHOT: Stone cairn and Monadnock view from Thumb Mountain

OWNERSHIP: Harris Center for Conservation Education

DIRECTIONS:

OTHER NEARBY MICROS:

- The Cadot Trail offers a shorter but steeper ascent of Mount Skatutakee and a chance to make another hike configuration of this loop.
- The East Side Trails starting at the Harris Center comprise another 4.5 miles of hiking (including a loop back on the road). The Channing Trail offers solitude, streams, and wetlands, while the Boulder Loop Trail is a one-mile round-trip hike that takes hikers past some of the most impressive boulder piles in the region.

MicroExploring Practices

Laughter

Just as sneezing and coughing are our body's automated ways to spew out unwelcome liquids, laughter is our way of releasing anxiety and repressed energies. If our intelligence is our engine, then laughter is our muffler—it's how we relieve ourselves of the seriousness of life and the coldness of logic. Laughing, it turns out, is quite a serious thing!

Nature Isn't Always Serious

No rule says that a walk in nature must be silent, stern, meditative, and scientific. In fact, it's the perfect setting to let go and be silly, especially when only the trees and birds are watching. MicroExploring is a prime time to deploy your full collection of corny dad jokes and become a kid again. Laughing is giving yourself space to let your system breathe and release some of the weight and seriousness of life.

Finding your laughter doesn't need to be limited to jokes and punch lines. Simple play can lead to joy. Talk to squirrels that seem extra chatty while they eat their nuts. Give them funny names or narrate their thoughts. Find unusually shaped trees or rocks that make for funny selfie photos. Jump from rock to rock over a stream, trying not to get wet, and make a game of it. Pick up and throw acorns (gently!) at your hiking companion. Try balancing on a fallen log like a tightrope walker, mimic bird calls (badly is funnier!), or have a race up a small, clear hill. Spontaneous and simple fun is good medicine.

Set the tone for humor from the beginning. Mutual laughter is the bonding glue of human connection, and making positive associations with nature will remind you that when you're outside you can relax and play, just like when you were a kid.

Silliness in nature is an expression of joy and has powerful medicinal effects.

I went to the woods because I wished to live deliberately.

—*Henry David Thoreau*

PARTRIDGE WOODS AND KULISH LEDGES

14

WALKING STICKS

Rugged Summits

Nelson

Hike Summary

The Partridge Woods property is one of the region's best-kept hiking secrets. An extensive high-elevation trail system explores stunning viewpoints, pleasant waterfalls, lost cellar holes, and diverse woodlands over a vast stretch of conserved land. Step onto its trails in search of its secret summits and natural treasures.

Highlights

- Hike to the headwaters of three different local watersheds—the Ashuelot River, the North Branch of the Contoocook River, and Nubanusit Brook
- Climb the SuperSanctuary's highest summit—Osgood Hill, at 2,233 feet
- Enjoy mountain and lake views in the heart of a conserved landscape
- Get a glimpse into Nelson's early history by peering into its cellar holes
- Discover awe-inspiring cascades and abundant spring blooms

Note: There are two ample parking lots for this extensive system of trails. For a point-to-point hike, leave a car on both ends. The trail from Brickyard Road offers a gentler ascent, but there are still plenty of climbs in that direction.

A visit to the charming village of Nelson is like stepping back in time.

Nelson (formerly known as Packersfield) is a particularly remote SuperSanctuary town with a small, rural population. Censuses from 1790 indicate a population of 721, which had grown by only thirteen residents by 2020. Its rocky terrain and lack of railroads have kept it off the beaten path. Thanks in no small part to its natural surroundings, a vibrant community of writers, artists, musicians, and craftspeople has germinated here and continues to have an outsized impact on the cultural heritage of the region.

Back in 1989, the Harris Center, still in its infancy as a land trust, purchased 108 acres encompassing what is now called Kulish Ledges. Thanks to several funding sources, the Harris

Center and the Town of Nelson expanded land protection efforts in 2016. The Nelson Conservation Commission and Nelson Trails Committee began to develop a connected trail network that spans several miles of wild, wooded hilltops.

These trails can be walked anytime, including winter, but a favorite time is during the "bronze age" of late autumn, when oak and beech leaves dominate, or "stick season," when bare trees open up several impressive views of different parts of the region. Summer's not bad either, especially when other mountain trails are crowded.

Bailey Brook Loop (2.1-mile loop)

Start at the Old Stoddard Road parking area along Priscilla's Path, an old logging road. There's a little falls on the right, and you enter a hardwood forest with dense hobblebush understory. Its heart-shaped leaves, appearing opposite on the branches, have attractive white flower clusters in spring and equally stunning fall foliage. The hobblebush used to be frequently browsed by moose, much less frequently now, as moose ticks have taken a toll on their hosts' population.

A well-built bridge crosses the spring-fed Bailey Brook. At the junction, take a left onto Holt Trail, marked in blue, and follow a babbling brook through young hardwoods, noticing the confluence of three streams. These lead to a series of beaver meadows, where mountain holly and other plants give it a northern feel. Look for several beaver dams and an overgrown beaver lodge, a mound next to the water. The vegetation atop the lodge indicates it's abandoned. A large marsh on the left features abundant birdlife, including alder flycatchers and

Black bears have left bite and scratch marks on this utility pole; hobblebush, here in its fall foliage, is often favored by moose for browsing.

common yellowthroats; yellow swamp candles bloom here in July. Notice the beaver dam's arched shape, built to withstand water pressure.

You'll come to a junction with the Kulish Ledges Trail. Stay left for the Holt Trail and venture to an interesting area with some lovely cascades, a historic dam, and old cellar holes. Meander around the wetland edge and past old bog bridges—the trail was built in a time of higher water. Cross another bridge, then through some recent logging on abutting land with isolated pines. Bear left at a woods road, following this short spur to a former trailhead at Old Stoddard Road. Follow this gravel road downhill (right) for a short stretch, watching for utility poles on which bears bite and scratch to leave their scent.

Watch for Bailey Brook Trail on the right, which is marked by the Nelson town trails' blackfly logo. Follow it past a view of the privately owned lower falls (please heed private property signage) and its narrow ten-foot cascade down a rock face, one of the region's prettiest roadside falls. Follow the brook up the trail, past several pools and cascades, to a beaver dam and small pond. There's a "lemon squeeze" feature between two boulders en route that is fun for kids and adults alike. After a footbridge comes another waterfall—the upper falls—and two parallel spurs (one labeled EASY WAY) from which to approach it. The Osborn Sawmill operated between 1815 and 1860 at the top of these falls, once home to a fifteen-foot overshot wheel nestled between two impressive parallel stone walls. Seasonal water flow here powered a saw, where according to local lore a man was cut in half long ago.

Continue on the Bailey Brook Trail (marked yellow), meandering along the brook, then onto a narrow cattle path between stone walls. Here, farm animals moved between a barn and stream. Atop this hill stood a house, the Osborn Homestead (1800), once perched prominently with views all around, but now well enclosed by woods. Take a right onto an unmarked woods road to see the cellar hole and stone well, and nearby a barn foundation. Try to imagine the hardships of life at the time it was inhabited. Volunteers try to keep the forest from swallowing this history completely. A former field next to the house is largely free of stones and thus was likely cultivated. Daylilies around the old homestead bloom in July. Despite their day-to-day challenges of survival, there was still room for beauty.

Continue along the unmarked woods road before rejoining the Holt Trail, returning the way you came. You may return to the parking lot or turn onto the Kulish Ledge Trail for a lengthier hike to its namesake ledge and Osgood Hill.

An oversize stone wall hints at this landscape's history: it's part of the foundation of the former Osborn Sawmill, which operated two hundred years ago.

The Viewpoints and Osgood Hill (4.2-mile loop)

From the trail junction with the Holt Trail, follow the yellow-blazed Kulish Ledge Trail steadily uphill, at times along a stone wall. This forest is dominated by northern hardwoods—white ash, sugar maple, and yellow birch, with plenty of red oaks, too—and its unbroken canopy and ferny understory create a contrast in size, scale, and color in summer or fall. Continue your climb, and eventually you'll notice something out of place along the path on the left—a rusty iron cookstove made by the Barstow Stove Company in 1836, complete with two cast-iron pots. One wonders whom it served and what purpose. Perhaps it and an associated structure, no longer present, supported a logging crew camped out here for some time.

The soil softens underfoot as spruces start to shade you. Blackburnian warblers and dark-eyed juncos sing in this forest type during summer. Traverse a series of blowdowns, the result of an unnamed wind event that seems to have been quite localized, perhaps a downburst in which trees were fanned out in all directions. Spruces give way to hardwoods again, and ledge outcrops become apparent as the slope steepens to your left.

The East Pinnacle viewpoint looks out across much of the Super-Sanctuary's conserved shorelines and summits.

Soon, a tremendous view opens up rather suddenly on the left. This is East Pinnacle, arguably the finest view of mountains and lakes in the SuperSanctuary. Virtually all the summits to the east can be seen—Bald, Skatutakee and Thumb, Crotched, the Wapacks, even the Pawtuckaway Mountains and points closer to the coast. You might glimpse turkey vultures or a bald eagle soaring below you here. While morning features full sun, you're shaded later in the day by the western cover.

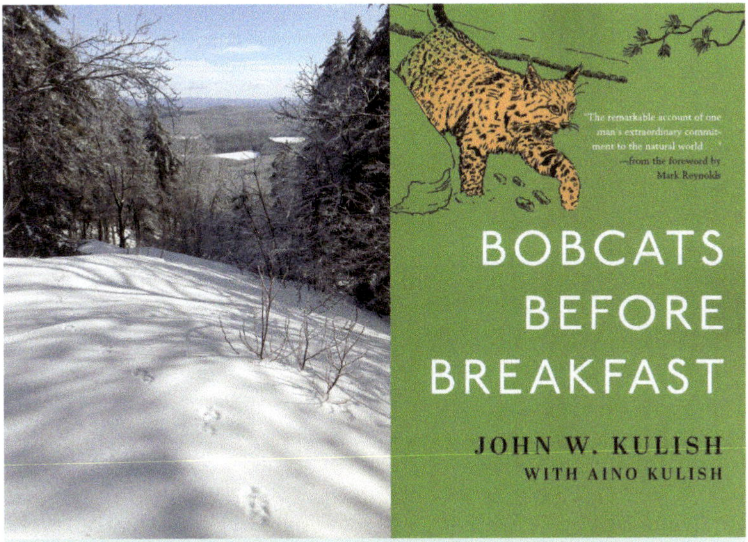

A former trapper who became a naturalist, John Kulish followed bobcats to the place that now bears his name. His book, *Bobcats Before Breakfast*, is full of lore from these hills.

After a long rest, continue in search of a different viewpoint. A north view on a short, unofficial spur leads to Patek's Point and its pocket view, where Mount Kearsarge and rolling hills are visible. There's a sprucy smell from here onward as you climb to Kulish Ledge, a prominent rocky spine of an east-facing ridgeline. From here, the view is more limited, but it features the corners of Nubanusit Lake and Spoonwood Pond. This location was named for John Kulish, a trapper-turned-naturalist who helped shape the Harris Center's outdoor education programs. John trekked all through the SuperSanctuary's hills in search of bobcats many decades ago. This local legend became a noted educator and trip leader for the Harris Center and eventually wrote a book titled *Bobcats Before Breakfast*. According to John, this ledge was one of the best for bobcats in the region.

The signpost atop Osgood Hill, the second-highest point in Cheshire County, suggests that this was once a busier place than it is today.

At a junction, follow the same trail (right) to Osgood Hill. This stretch remains shaded under a cool, fragrant canopy of spruce. Next is a slow ascent to the summit of Osgood Hill, which, at 2,233 feet in elevation, is the second-highest summit in Cheshire

County. At one thousand feet lower than Monadnock and essentially viewless, it's a very different experience from the more famous mountain. Here, a signpost marks the distances to the various trailheads and hilltops. This summit was formerly called City Hill because quite a few homesteads once topped this gentle rise. A canopy of oaks, maples, and cherry trees now stands in their place. At the next junction is a decision point—loop back, or continue onto Hurd Hill, Blacktop, and Brickyard Road. To return, follow the Holt Trail (blue), then stay right where the Ridge Trail (orange) comes in from the left. The return trip down on either of these beautiful ridgeline trails contains its own viewpoints and secrets. There are cellar holes, big trees, wild lowbush blueberries, owl woods, and more that your boots and mind may wander to.

A bit of effort is required to get to these trails. The remoteness allows you to go deep—in distance, history, and your own self-discovery.

Photo by Tom Momeyer

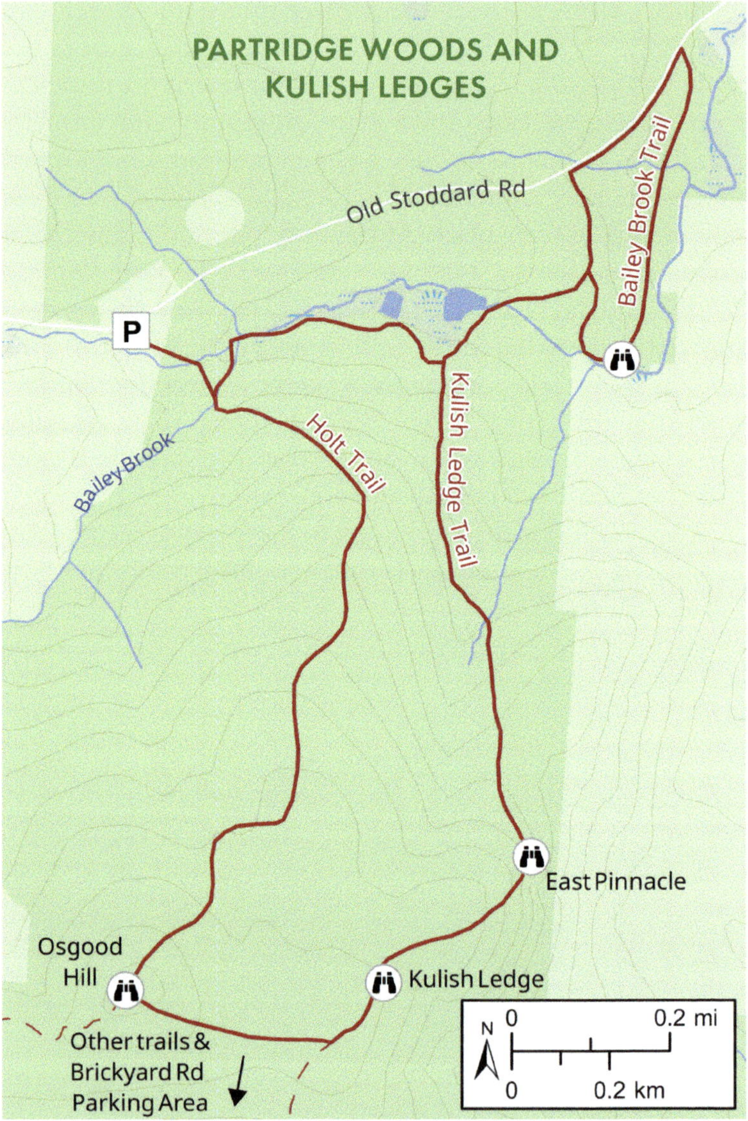
PARTRIDGE WOODS AND
KULISH LEDGES
Old Stoddard Rd
P
Bailey Brook Trail
Kulish Ledge Trail
Holt Trail
Bailey Brook
East Pinnacle
Osgood
Hill
Kulish Ledge
Other trails &
Brickyard Rd
Parking Area
N
0
0.2 mi
0
0.2 km

Lay of the Land

TRAILS: 8.9 miles of moderate to challenging hiking over some steep and rugged terrain connecting the two parking areas on various trails

ACCESS: Parking areas along Old Stoddard Road and Brickyard Road

PERMITTED USES: Foot traffic only; dogs are welcome, as are mountain bikes; hunting is permitted

A GREAT PLACE TO: Look out over broad lake and mountain views

INSIDER TIP: Hike the ridgeline during stick season

DON'T MISS: The view from Kulish Ledges

CREATURE FEATURE: Bobcat

TREASURE HUNT: The old Barstow stove along the Kulish Ledges Trail

FAVORITE MONTH: November

SNAPSHOT: East Pinnacle viewpoint

OWNERSHIP: Town of Nelson and the Harris Center; trails managed by the Nelson Conservation Commission and Nelson Trails Committee

DIRECTIONS:

Old Stoddard Road

Brickyard Road

MicroExploring Practices

Walking Sticks

There's a misconception that walking sticks are only for the elderly or those with mobility issues. Some believe they're solely for intense, challenging hikes. But the humble walking stick is the unsung hero of the trail. The stick is a companion, a tool, and a source of both physical and psychological support. We've become so accustomed to walking sticks—the weight in our hands, the rhythm they create with each step—that hiking without one feels strangely incomplete, as if something critical is missing.

The walking stick is the humble, unsung hero of the trail.

Some people use commercial lightweight hiking poles, but despite all of their useful merits for hiking, they're just not the same as sticks fallen from trees and dried out naturally. Personalizing your walking stick is an act of self-expression; I add trinkets and markings, paint parts of them, or attach fabric scraps from old scarves or shirts. There's nothing wrong with injecting a little magic and creative spirit into your experiences in nature. The goal is to fashion something that feels good and powerful in your hands.

From the moment you begin your hike, holding a stick reawakens the sense of touch—a sense so often forgotten in our screen-bound, sterile routines. There is a certain comfort in its texture, in the sound it makes as it taps the ground. Its rhythm brings us right back to our roots in these forests as more primitive beings. As you move, the stick becomes a subconscious extension of yourself, offering a feeling of protection. It allows you to relax into your walk, knowing you have an extra layer of support.

Your Body Thanks the Stick

Beyond the sense of companionship and connection, the humble walking stick offers tangible physical rewards that truly enhance the hiking experience. That extra point of contact with the ground becomes a reliable anchor, providing welcome stability on uneven terrain riddled with roots or loose stones, significantly reducing the risk of a tumble and boosting your confidence with every step. You'll feel the difference especially on descents, as the stick helps absorb impact and distribute your weight, lessening the strain on hardworking knees, ankles, and hips.

It's more than just a support for balance; using a stick incorporates your upper body into the rhythm of the walk. This gentle engagement provides a light workout for your arms, shoulders, and core, building strength and helping reduce fatigue in your legs.

Your posture will improve from a more upright and balanced stance as you move through the woods with a stick. Without one, your eyes naturally drop toward the ground, constantly scanning each step. But with a stick, your balance is more secure, and your gaze is freer to lift. You look up more often, which allows your mind to absorb the landscape instead of just the terrain beneath your feet.

Walking with a stick signals to your mind that you are not just walking—you are exploring. It shifts your mindset from a simple stroll into a deliberate adventure.

ROBB RESERVOIR PADDLE 15

PEACEFUL PADDLES

Wild Waters

Stoddard

Photo by Tom Momeyer

If there is magic on this planet, it is contained in water.

—Loren Eiseley

Paddle Summary

Near the headwaters of the North Branch of the Contoocook in Stoddard, a protected pond provides some of the finest and most remote flat-water paddling in the region. Robb Reservoir, Rye Pond, and North Branch Pond (also known as Compass Pond) are impoundments that fluctuate between pond and marsh, depending on the season and water levels. They are home to interesting and rare plant communities as well as an expansive refuge for uncommon wildlife species.

Highlights

- Search for river otters and moose in their choicest habitat
- Spot ducks and other water birds as you explore marshy coves
- Enjoy big views of pristine water and undeveloped mountains in a conserved landscape
- Admire the abundance of pond lilies and be mesmerized by the swirling masses of whirligig beetles
- Listen for the chorus of frogs and toads and the songs of scarlet tanagers and warblers
- Enjoy "idle productivity" as you drift and float, letting your mind wander and wonder

Paddlers setting out to explore Robb Reservoir by boat.

These ponds are connected by the North Branch, a river with its own wild character. Few people see this stretch, which contains both calmer and faster-flowing sections. Of the places to paddle, Robb Reservoir is perhaps the choice flat-water section. The reservoir is named for Christopher Robb, a local business owner (and early proponent of sustainable forest management) who opened the Stoddard Lumber Mill in the 1850s and built the first dam here to power it. It's a ninety-five-acre oasis of wildness. Despite its ease of access (it's close to the highway, and it's easy to park and unload), Robb Reservoir is seldom crowded and offers an abundance of marshy edges, islands, wildlife, and peace. It's a two-hour ambitious paddle to cover its entirety, but set aside more time if you like to dawdle and drift.

Spring conditions give Robb the appearance of a northern lake, but at just nine feet in depth, it's choked with lilies by July and feels more like a large marsh. A well-defined and meandering channel of the "river" becomes apparent in these conditions; outside it, you might encounter the drag of pondweeds and lilies. Warm-water fish species like bass and pickerel are present if you want to try your luck. Birders frequently enjoy plentiful waterfowl in spring and fall migrations, and herons, ospreys, and kingfishers throughout the paddling seasons. Boasting an abundance of wildlife into October, Robb may be at its finest during fall foliage time, when red maples ring the pond, contrasting with darker greens of pines, hemlocks, and spruce.

Autumn paddling is one of the great joys of MicroExploring the SuperSanctuary.

A Juxtaposition of Wildness and Progress

Robb offers a visual barrier from Route 9, but you can still often hear it, especially during rush hours and on busy summer weekends. The sound is a reminder of how close this special place was to losing its wild character. For three decades, local conservationists and the Town of Stoddard fought proposals to develop the shoreline. In 2006, an eighty-two-unit subdivision plan proposed by a developer finally brought the funds to the table. Thanks to considerable federal, state, and local support, the Harris Center acquired the property for $3.9 million in 2007, permanently conserving 1,668 acres of wetland and upland habitats—a huge success for conservation interests. What's more, its acquisition linked conserved landscapes in southwestern New Hampshire—thirteen thousand acres to the north and twenty-seven thousand acres to the south—providing vital connectivity for the movement of wide-ranging wildlife species, and, in hindsight, allowing for climate migration in a warming world.

Road noise aside, Robb remains a hidden gem. The scenery at Robb is spectacular and changes as you paddle out the long straightaway, which opens up magically to the main part of the pond, marshier and wider. It features a view of several of the SuperSanctuary's highest hills, including Osgood Hill and Rollstone Mountain. Notice Bald Mountain and its ridgeline, hiding Willard Pond in its shadows. It could be a Canadian backdrop.

Wildlife Abounds in the Coves

When you reach the bend, paddle partway into a cove on the right. A deeper river corridor meanders through a sea of pond lilies of different shapes and sizes. By early July, decomposers have already taken a toll, and yellows and browns of these decaying leaves add to the beauty and color of the scene. Be sure to drift and watch the hordes of swirling whirligig beetles (you'll know them when you see them!). Named for their incessant, mesmerizing, circular gyrations in large groups as they feed on the surface, they are thought to congregate for safety. We challenge you to follow just one with your eye as long as you can.

It's hard not to be awed by the symmetrical beauty of a blooming white water lily. Look more closely and you may see visiting insects as well.

Photo by Tom Momeyer

Back in the main channel of the reservoir, notice a triangular rock by a point where a wood duck nest box is mounted, perhaps by birders or hunters. Both groups work together to promote waterfowl conservation initiatives, which were helpful in funding the acquisition of habitat here. Wood ducks, mergansers, teals, and other water birds may take off from a shallow cove of spatterdock—the large yellow pond lilies. Be aware that waterfowl hunting occurs here in the fall, managed by the New Hampshire Fish and Game Department, the state entity that also manages the dam and water resources.

A great blue heron lands itself a fine meal: a large brook trout.
Photo by Brian Reilly

Another cove contains a shoreline beaver lodge sprawled around a narrow peninsula, where a natural stone dock makes a fine place to stretch the legs and take a pit stop. There's an art to docking on a natural feature where only rocks and logs meet you on the shoreline. On this island, you're hidden in plain sight, protected by the vast solitude.

Tune in to the abundance of birdsong that dominates between May and July. Among those audible are baby red-winged blackbirds begging from the marsh shrubs, along with the adults' "*kon-ka-ree*." Overhead, the bouncy songs of American goldfinches seem to imitate their trampolining flight. The happy chatter of chickadees, jingling of downy woodpeckers, and nasal yanking of nuthatches—on either side of the coves—are all parts of a bigger conversation. Try to decipher bird language, even if you don't know all the songs.

Coves call out in every direction, each with secrets to share. Maybe you'll come upon a moose taking a drink, or more likely, witness an otter family following fish above and below the surface. On the return trip, turn back to glimpse the very tip of a shining white object that seems to slash the hillside—a wind turbine from the Tuttle Hill facility, and one of just two human-made features in view on this pond. It's easy to ignore them or miss them completely.

An aerial view of Robb Reservoir shows a well-defined river channel.
Photo by James Newsom

The Return

Bear right to stay in the sun and maintain big views, following the sinuous waterway, or stay left to find a rocky shoreline and the narrow shortcut you can only discover by boat. Back around the cove to the long straightaway, keep an eye on the massive shoreline boulder most of the way back to the launch, your North Star to guide you back in. Your destination now in sight, drift at a leisurely pace or paddle steadily, depending upon what you need.

Beyond Robb

Compass Pond (reached 1.25 miles farther along the private road past the turnoff to Robb) and the North Branch of the Contoocook River (best at high water) are also great paddling options.

To see a list of our favorite paddling spots in the SuperSanctuary, click on the QR code to the right.

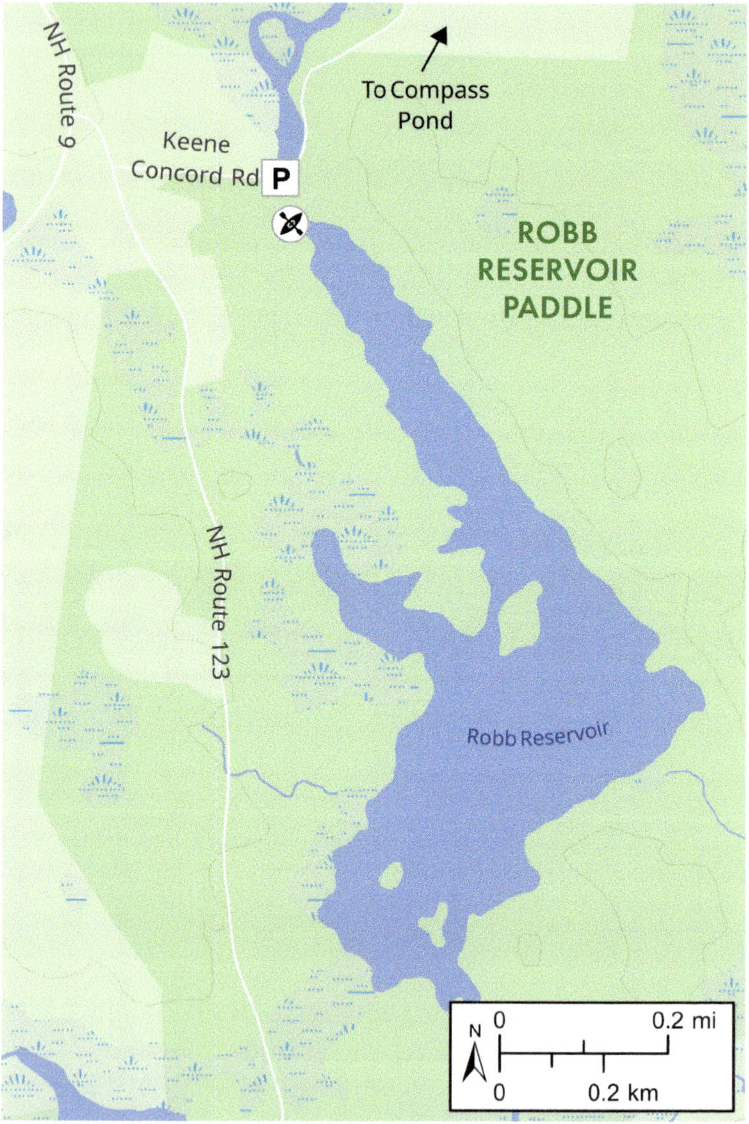
NH Route 9
To Compass Pond
Keene Concord Rd
P
ROBB RESERVOIR PADDLE
NH Route 123
Robb Reservoir
N
0
0.2 mi
0
0.2 km

Lay of the Land

ACCESS: Parking area on Keene Concord Road in Stoddard off Route 123 (high-clearance vehicles recommended)

PERMITTED USES: Canoeing, kayaking, fishing, hunting, swimming, hiking, cross-country skiing, and snowshoeing

A GREAT PLACE TO: Escape to a wild waterway

INSIDER TIP: Explore the little islands in the lake

DON'T MISS: Fall foliage from a pond

CREATURE FEATURE: River otter

TREASURE HUNT: The inlet of the North Branch River near the far end of Robb Reservoir

FAVORITE MONTH: July

SNAPSHOT: Macro view of a sea of pond lilies

OWNERSHIP: Harris Center for Conservation Education and the State of New Hampshire

DIRECTIONS:

MicroExploring Practices

Peaceful Paddles

The SuperSanctuary is blessed with an abundance of water—ponds, lakes, streams, and rivers, all waiting for exploration, many of them easy to access. Some are big enough for day-long paddles, others so small you can circle them in under an hour. Each offers a different experience and kind of intimacy with its natural surroundings. There's a certain irreplaceable beauty that can only be found while on the water in a canoe or kayak. If you observe patiently and intentionally, the water will come alive. It is living art. As substrate, the water takes many forms. It glistens or reflects, flows or chops. The shoreline bends differently from the seat of a canoe, distorting distance. Sounds carry across the water in mysterious ways. The dip of your paddle punctuates silence, forming ripples and tiny whirlpools.

Seasons on the Water

Each season on the water offers its own reward. Spring brings cold, clear water and an abundance of birds, insects, and plant life returning to the water's edge. It's also a chance to paddle marshy wetlands that may be dry or choked with vegetation by late summer. Summer features long days, satisfying swims, carefree sounds of the season, and the glow of a warm sun. Come August, there's no better place to be. Fall is heralded by crimson maples and auburn oaks contrasting with greens of pine, hemlock, and spruce, all of it reflected in still water—a final blaze of color before the lakes grow quiet again.

Spiritual Escape

Paddling can be a form of exercise, but you don't need to work hard to reap its benefits. Sometimes the benefits are more spiritual. Drifting across a pond or marsh is a good reminder that there's no shame in being idle. Stillness of body can activate the mind. Let your thoughts drift as your boat does. Time on the water restores an inner calm. You allow peace to enter your being with every stroke of the paddle. To drift, to float, to pause in the center of a pond and listen—this is one of the most reliable medicines the outdoors can offer.

Closer to Nature

Paddling offers a closer approach to wildlife, and you'll see and hear more when you're still or passively drifting. Bask in the serenade of nature's soundscapes—birds, frogs, insects, and more. Move slowly and quietly toward turtles on logs, kingfishers on shoreline trees, and other natural features that have always seemed alluring from land but are now within reach. Despite the proximity to nature, an added reason to take to the water (especially in spring and summer) is to escape pesky insects, often kept away by a light breeze.

A simple canoe or kayak unlocks the region's endless chain of lakes and ponds. They offer a rare way to experience true movement and deep stillness all at once.

The Hardest Part

Let's admit it: The toughest part of canoeing or kayaking is almost always the loading and unloading. Wrestling the boat onto a roof rack or dragging it down a short embankment feels like the price of admission, but some places have more accessible launches. Regardless, once you've pushed off, the effort is forgotten. What follows is pure bliss—an experience that asks nothing of you but to move slowly, breathe deeply, and glide. Make your own trail on the water, and go at your own speed.

On the water, discovery comes easy. You don't need an expedition. A single hour before sunset on a nearby pond can feel like a small journey into another world. Escape from—and to—the "real world" for a little while in your kayak or canoe, where no two journeys are alike.

A Few More Paddling Pointers

- Try a point-to-point paddle, with cars at each end and a friend along for the adventure.
- Make a practice of paddling ponds you've never been to before.
- Bring creature comforts: a comfortable seat, delicious food and drinks, lightweight paddles.
- Don't forget the basics: sun protection, a wide-brimmed hat, warm clothes, and personal flotation devices.

CONSERVATION PARTNERS

Without the stewardship and leadership of the Harris Center and many other private and public conservation groups operating in this region, there would be no SuperSanctuary. These champions include local land trusts, statewide organizations, towns, the state and federal government, and private landowners, as well as generous individuals who have provided support.

But conservation, expansive and expanding as it is, doesn't automatically mean that the lands and waters are free from threats and changes. This takes monitoring, stewardship, and love—which grows out of a deep connection to a place. We need it today, more than ever, to face the slew of changes on our doorstep. Invasive species and storms, exacerbated by a changing climate, stewardship-related actions such as logging, as well as development, land use changes, and more, are pressures that will alter what we know and have come to love. But in these changes, many of which are coming faster than before, there is an opportunity to learn, to study, to continue to steward and love. Conservation isn't a one-time act. It's an ongoing relationship. And relationships require presence. Our sense of place—our ability to know these wild places at all and our appreciation for them—depends upon those who continue to care for them, clear their trails, monitor them, and protect them.

The following list of partners, while not comprehensive, includes many of the groups responsible for conserving and stewarding SuperSanctuary lands:

The **Andorra Forest** has been actively managed for timber, wildlife, recreation, and water for generations and includes the 2,650-acre Wildcat Hollow Wilderness Area.

The **Beech Hill–Dublin Lake Watershed Association** was formed in 2005 to protect Dublin Lake and the natural resources of Beech Hill. The association supports the preservation of Dublin Lake and its watershed and promotes activities to further land and watershed protection goals.

Bennington Conservation Commission https://www.townofbennington.com/conservationcommission

Since its inception, the **Crotched Mountain Foundation**, one of New England's most iconic nonprofit organizations, has worked toward one goal: helping children, students, and adults with disabilities to live, learn, and thrive in the community. https://www.cmf.org/trails

Dublin Conservation Commission https://www.townofdublin.org/conservation-commission

Greenfield Conservation Commission https://www.greenfield-nh.gov/conservation-commission

Hancock Conservation Commission https://www.hancocknh.org/boards_committees/a_m/conservation_commission/index.php

The **Harris Center for Conservation Education**, a donor-supported, nonprofit organization, is a transformative force in the Monadnock region that promotes understanding and respect for the natural world through education for people of all ages, direct protection and exemplary stewardship of the region's natural resources, conservation research, and programs that encourage active participation in the great outdoors. https://www.harriscenter.org

Harrisville Conservation Commission https://harrisvillenh.org/government/conservation-commission

As a land trust for southwestern New Hampshire, the **Monadnock Conservancy**'s mission is to work with communities and landowners to conserve the natural resources, wild and working lands, rural character, and scenic beauty of the Monadnock region. https://www.monadnockconservancy.org

The mission of the **Nature Conservancy** is to conserve the lands and waters on which all life depends. Together with partners, local landowners, and the support of members, they have helped protect nearly three hundred thousand acres and 680 miles of rivers and streams in New Hampshire since 1961. https://www.nature.org/newhampshire

Nelson Conservation Commission https://www.townofnelson.org/conservation-commission

New Hampshire Audubon, an independent nonprofit established in 1914, is dedicated to the protection of New Hampshire's natural environment for wildlife and people. With forty wildlife sanctuaries and three centers, New Hampshire Audubon focuses on wildlife conservation research, wildlife habitat management, environmental policy, and environmental education. https://www.nhaudubon.org

New Hampshire Fish and Game Department https://www.wildlife.nh.gov

New Hampshire State Parks https://www.nhstateparks.org

Peterborough Conservation Commission https://www.peterboroughnh.gov/government/boards_and_committees/conservation_commission/index.php

Town of Peterborough https://www.peterboroughnh.gov

Founded by a handful of concerned citizens in 1901, the **Society for the Protection of New Hampshire Forests** is one of the country's most effective statewide land conservation organizations, dedicated to protecting New Hampshire's most important landscapes while promoting the wise use of its renewable natural resources. https://www.forestsociety.org

Stoddard Conservation Commission https://www.stoddardnh.org/conservation-commission

FURTHER RESOURCES

Here are some suggestions for further reading and listening:

Anderson, Dave, and Chris Martin. *Something Wild.* New Hampshire Public Radio. Recurring segment, also available as a podcast. https://www.nhpr.org/show/something-wild.

Goodby, Robert G. *A Deep Presence: 13,000 Years of Native American History.* Peter E. Randall, 2021.

Holland, Mary. *Naturally Curious: A Photographic Field Guide and Month-by-Month Journey Through the Fields, Woods, and Marshes of New England.* Trafalgar Square, 2010. https://www.naturallycuriouswithmaryholland.wordpress.com/about.

iNaturalist. https://www.inaturalist.org.

Northern Woodlands Magazine. Center for Northern Woodlands Education. https://www.northernwoodlands.org.

Von Mertens, Francie. *Nature Almanac and Calendar: Nature Observed in the Backyard and Beyond.* Harris Center for Conservation Education, 2020.

Wessels, Thomas. *Reading the Forested Landscape: A Natural History of New England.* Norton, 1997.

ACKNOWLEDGMENTS

This book grew out of many footsteps, shared conversations, and quiet hours spent along the trails, paths, and waters of the Monadnock region. Our deepest gratitude goes to our first major supporter, Eleanor Briggs, who believed in our vision and who has spent a lifetime creating sanctuary for all.

Along with her, we thank our major supporters: Meade Cadot and Sandy Taylor, Chuck and Kris Carlson, Francie Von Mertens, Michael and Cathy George, Nina and Archie McIntyre, Dennis and Fran Brown, William Deal, and Travis Topa and Christy Keefe, as well as all of our patrons for supporting this project.

We thank the staff, volunteers, and supporters of all the conservation organizations in the SuperSanctuary who dedicate themselves daily to the land they protect and the community they inspire. Special thanks to Meade Cadot and Susie Spikol, who shared stories and suggestions, and to the Harris Center, which supported our first steps and continues to champion our efforts.

We're grateful to the incredibly talented professionals we've worked with in the creation of this book: our talented and passionate book designers, Michelle Aldredge and Corwin Levi from Gwarlingo Studio, who guided us confidently through unknown terrain; editor John Knight, for challenging us and helping us climb higher; copy editor Hannah Mahoney, for combing through every word, posing thoughtful questions, and proposing solutions to topical issues; proofreader Henry Walters, our friend and fellow explorer, for his careful review and keen eye; mapmaker Nate Marchessault, who carefully designed the functional and attractive maps throughout; videographer Oriana Camara, who, through her lens, captured the essence of the book and made us look really good! Finally, this book would be nowhere without our incredible project manager and friend, Tim Ditlow, who was a pillar of this project from beginning to end. Tim has been a masterful communicator, cheerleader, voice of reason, and taskmaster, and he helped us create the highest-quality book we could ever have dreamed of.

We appreciate all the individuals and organizational stewards within the SuperSanctuary, who welcomed us into these green spaces and shared their unique stories, especially Joe MacGregor (Bennington Conservation Commission), Nina McIntyre, Archie McIntyre, and Peter Kenyon (Beech Hill–Dublin Lake Watershed Association), Marc Nutter (New Hampshire Audubon), Eric Aldrich, Joanne Glode and Megan Latour (the Nature Conservancy), Anne McBride and Janine Marr (Monadnock Conservancy), Zach Pearo and Annie Faulkner (Andorra Forest), Eric Masterson, Jeremy Wilson, and Brett Amy Thelen (the Harris Center), Al Stoops and Kathy Schillemat (Nelson Trails Committee), Geri Bailey (Stoddard Conservation Commission), Alan Rumrill, Kevin Harte and Rick Fife (Crotched Mountain Foundation), Matt Scaccia, Dave Anderson, Steve Junkin, Ian Aldrich, and Wendy Weisiger (Forest Society), Swift Corwin, and Tom Eid. Thanks to all who contributed beautiful and illustrative photos: Chuck Carlson, Meade Cadot, Ben Conant, Brian Reilly, Tom Momeyer, James Newsom, Brett Amy Thelen, Susan Kline, Julie Brown, Frank Gorga, Kate McKay, and Lucy Zukaitis.

Thanks as well to our friends and many fellow wanderers who joined us on MicroExploring walks and shared their sense of wonder or key guidance, especially Glenn, Paul, Dan, Cheryl, Henry, Katrina, Levi, Kelly, Jesse, Kim, Ross, Joslin, Matt, Sy, Will, Tom, Laura, Jer, Chris, Kate, Steven, Chad, Will, Emma, Rich, Anne, and Brett.

Thank you to our families and loved ones for their encouragement and understanding throughout the long process of bringing this project to life. To Julie, for her love and support, and for often baking sweet treats for the hungry writers. To our beloved children, Laurel, Amalia, and Alden, for accompanying us on many of our adventures in "the Dadlands," for carrying forth these treasured memories in their own ways, and for their patience and enthusiasm as we balanced time to scout, write, and create.

Finally, we acknowledge the land itself and its wild creatures for being our guides—teaching us patience, observation, and listening, and helping cultivate a most valuable friendship.

INDEX

A

B

C

D

E

F

G

H

O

P

R

S

T

ABOUT THE AUTHORS

PHIL BROWN is a lifelong birder, a trained naturalist, and an experienced guide whose passion for the wild finds its truest expression outdoors when shared person to person, in forests, wetlands, and mountain ridges across and beyond the SuperSanctuary. As bird conservation director for the Harris Center for Conservation Education, Phil leads programs that connect people with the land and its wild things through observation, stewardship, and wonder. He has guided countless field trips, written extensively about New England's birdlife and sense of place, and leads and collaborates on research and conservation projects throughout the region. Phil has lived in and around the SuperSanctuary for many years and now resides in Hancock, New Hampshire, with his wife, Julie; their two children, Laurel and Alden; a dog, Maggie; and a lively flock of chickens. His favorite MicroExplorations begin just outside his back door, where he has documented more than 160 species of wild birds.

IGNACIO OREAMUNO is a writer, artist, coffee amante, master mixologist, guide, and creative manifester whose work invites people to create a better world by slowing down, savoring life, and connecting to their personal dreams. His profound, deep sense of wonder channels into guiding others toward what is authentic and inspiring. He is the founder of The Dreamcatchers, a travel company that designs journeys of reflection, connection, and personal growth. Ignacio is also the author of *The Quiet Brand: The Introverted Future of Marketing*. Born in Costa Rica and now based in the deep forests of New Hampshire, he lives in Hancock with his dear daughter, Amalia, and a bearded dragon named Eclipse.